D0162685

WITHDRAWN

THE EVOLUTION OF
SCHOOL
DISTURBANCE
IN AMERICA

THE EVOLUTION OF SCHOOL DISTURBANCE IN AMERICA

Colonial Times to Modern Day

Gordon A. Crews and M. Reid Counts

Westport, Connecticut
London

Library of Congress Cataloging-in-Publication Data

Crews, Gordon A.
   The evolution of school disturbance in America : colonial times to
modern day / Gordon A. Crews and M. Reid Counts.
      p.   cm.
   Includes bibliographical references and index.
   ISBN 0–275–95842–6 (alk. paper)
   1. School violence—United States—History. 2. Education—Social
aspects—United States—History. 3. School management and
organization—United States—History. I. Counts, M. Reid, 1970–
. II. Title.
LB3013.3.C74   1997
371.5'8'0973—dc21   97–5582

British Library Cataloguing in Publication Data is available.

Library of Congress Catalog Card Number: 97–5582
ISBN: 0–275–95842–6

First published in 1997

Praeger Publishers, 88 Post Road West, Westport, CT 06881
An imprint of Greenwood Publishing Group, Inc.

Printed in the United States of America

The paper used in this book complies with the
Permanent Paper Standard issued by the National
Information Standards Organization (Z39.48–1984).

10 9 8 7 6 5 4 3 2

To my family: my wife, Pamela Player Crews; my son, Garrison Allen Crews; and my daughter, Samantha Leigh Crews.

G.A.C.

To my grandparents: Jetta Yates Dearman, Frances Ruff Counts, Edward Wheeler Counts, Sr., and in loving memory of Joe Reid Dearman.

M.R.C.

"For we must consider that we shall be a city upon a hill. The eyes of all people are upon us."

— John Winthrop, 1630

Contents

Preface

Two beliefs about education can be stated with almost absolute certainty. First, U.S. schools mirror U.S. society. As behaviors and attitudes change in society, so will they in education. Second, education in the United States has always followed a course directed by the prominent social developments of the time. Any significant change in U.S. schooling can be directly attributed to a change in social philosophy of that time. A third statement, perhaps more debatable than the preceeding two, is that education has always been asked to solve problems that it did not create in social environments that it cannot control. Evidence to support these three ideas can be found in any period of U.S. history.

PURPOSE OF WORK

In determining educational practices for their schools, policy makers, educators, and parents must often find their way through myriad conventions, recommendations, and theories. Much of this information is, in reality, misinformation, based on prejudice, lack of knowledge, fear, panic, opinions, and individual biased perspectives.

If the United States is ever to improve education and training to meet the ambitious national education goals, research must inform and encourage the development of sound policies and practices by making available, in a clear and understandable format, the most comprehensive information that is available. This work seeks to add to this body of knowledge and offer additional information for future research and educational efforts.

LIMITATIONS

Collecting data on school disturbance in U.S. history is difficult and sometimes misleading because:

no system for recording and enumerating individual acts existed until 1933, when the Federal Bureau of Investigation's Uniform Crime Report was developed;

many forms of individual aggression, such as juvenile misbehavior, were not a matter of public concern and attention until the 1960s;

throughout history, definitions of what constituted school disturbance have varied;

reporting procedures varied, and continue to vary, among school districts;

not until the 1970s did many school districts keep comprehensive data on student criminality;

local school administrators have historically played down their problems to preserve the impression that they controlled their school situations;

most early information on school disturbance and problems is primarily anecdotal or simply not available;

even the very definition of "school" has changed over time.

With this said, the following work is an attempt to provide the reader with the most comprehensive examination of the historical aspects of school disturbance possible.

Acknowledgments

I acknowledge the following for their support and guidance: Harvey A. Allen, without whom my research in school disturbance would never have begun; Mildred Vasan, without whom this book would not have been possible; James T. Sabin at Greenwood Publishing Group, for his efforts in this work; Ellen Dorosh for her efforts in the final production of this book; Chris Plyler and Lila Meeks for their confidence and support; and Reid H. Montgomery, Jr., who has been my close friend and mentor for many years.

I also offer my thanks and love to my parents, Gordon and Joyce Crews; my in-laws, Paul and Jean Player; and again to my family, Pam, Garris, and Samantha, for making it all worthwhile.

G.A.C.

A work such as this cannot be undertaken and completed successfully without the cooperation of many friends and colleagues. For their support I would like to thank my coauthor, Gordon A. Crews, for inviting me to participate in this project; Mildred Vasan and Praeger Publishers; Alan Wieder, for his patience; and my colleagues Cole Blease Graham, Jr.; Ellis C. MacDougal; William J. Mathias; James G. Fraser; and Karen A. Hutto.

For their love and guidance I thank my family and special friends: my parents Dinah and Steve Long, and Buddy and Connie Counts;

my siblings D'anne Long and Zack Counts; C. Shawn Galloway and Leigh Anne Bost.

M.R.C.

Introduction

In 1989, President George Bush and the nation's 50 governors held a historic education summit that culminated in the adoption of the U.S. national education goals, which were intended to serve as a framework for future reform efforts. The sixth of the U.S. national education goals states:

By the year 2000, every school in America will be free of drugs and violence and will offer a disciplined environment conducive to learning. The stated objectives are: Every school will implement a firm and fair policy on use, possession, and distribution of drugs and alcohol. Parents, businesses, and community organizations will work together to ensure that schools are a safe haven for all children. Every school district will develop a comprehensive K-12 drug and alcohol prevention education program. Drug and alcohol curriculum should be taught as an integral part of health education. In addition, community-based teams should be organized to provide students and teachers with needed support. (*Goals 2000*, 1991, p. 2)

This has been an ambitious objective for the United States. It has been estimated that a total of $91.48 million was allocated for the 50 states, Washington, D.C., and Puerto Rico for efforts to obtain the goals of Goals 2000 ($86.48 million for systemic reform state grants and $5 million for technology planning state grants). In 1995, President Clinton requested $700 million in his budget proposal to be administered by the U.S.

Department of Education and $12 million for the U.S. Department of Labor to support the National Skill Standards Board.

Because of the increases in reports of crime in society and violence in schools, it seems that the United States is making uncertain progress toward this goal. The spiraling increase in crime and violence has also caused many to question the safety of their neighborhoods and schools.

1

School Disturbance in U.S. Society

Any discussion of the evolution of school disturbance since the early colonial days in the United States will benefit from a brief overview of the history of school disturbance and violence.

Juvenile delinquency dates back to the beginning of recorded history. There have been many changes over the centuries in the types, amount, and suspected causes of delinquent behavior and what should be done to control the problem.

Among the Romans and Greeks, younger persons were not held responsible for the crimes they committed. The same point of view prevailed in the Napoleonic Code. In English jurisprudence, however, there was little differentiation among children, youths, and adults until relatively modern times. The Chancery Courts of England were sometimes used for special legal processes, including cases involving children. Not until 1899 would there be a special court in the United States for juveniles (Barnes, 1972).

Throughout the Middle Ages and as late as the seventeenth century, children participated in acts that, if committed in modern times, would result in not only their being defined as delinquent but also in requiring their parents and other adults to be charged with contributing to their delinquency. As soon as they could talk, most children learned and used obscene language and gestures; many engaged in sexual activity at an early age, willingly or otherwise; they drank freely in taverns, if not at home; few of them ever went to school, and when they did, they wore sidearms, participated in brawls, and fought duels (Newman, 1980).

As a socially accepted concept of childhood grew and expanded, the meanings attached to it significantly altered. The acts of children that in previous centuries were not seen as particularly deviant suddenly became unique problems. New norms and expectations developed as childhood became a special phase in the life cycle (Newman, 1980). In this phase, school violence would find its origin.

Interestingly, the earliest reports of school violence focused on violence committed by teachers against their students, or what came to be called corporal punishment. In the seventeenth century, Jesuit schools expected their teachers to physically discipline their students. Serious offenders were stripped in front of the whole community and beaten until they bled. Whipping was considered a teaching aid (Regoli & Hewitt, 1994).

One of the foremost authorities on the subject of delinquency and its historical development was LaMar T. Empey. In 1978, Empey released documentation that indicated that violence among juveniles had characterized every era of recorded history since medieval periods (Regoli & Hewitt, 1994).

EXTENT OF SCHOOL DISTURBANCE IN THE UNITED STATES

Even as government officials, political candidates, and law enforcement officials across the country press for stronger anticrime measures, national statistical reports continue to show a decrease in almost all types of reported crime. The U.S. public does not attend to these reports. The amount of crime might be stabilizing, but crime still remains at a staggering level. The same reports show an increase in random violence and a decline in the ages of the perpetrators, which may explain why public fear has continued to increase.

According to the U.S. Department of Justice's Office of Juvenile Justice and Delinquency Prevention (1991), juveniles accounted for 17 percent of all arrests for violent crime in 1991. Juvenile arrests for murder increased by 85 percent between 1987 and 1991, and juvenile arrests for weapons violations increased 62 percent. Three of every 10 juvenile murder arrests in 1991 involved a victim under the age of 18. One out of five weapons arrests in 1991 was a juvenile arrest. Black youth were arrested for weapons-law violations at a rate triple that of white youth in 1991; they were victims of homicides at a rate six times higher than whites.

In any given year across the United States, approximately 100,000 children take guns to their schools each day, and 160,000 miss school because of fear of injury. On average, in each hour of the school day, 2,000 young people are attacked by other students, 900 teachers will be threatened, and another 400 teachers will be attacked. At homes and in communities, approximately every 36 minutes one child is killed or injured by a firearm for an average of more than 14,000 each year (National Center for Education Statistics, 1994).

In 1991, the students in K–12 education most often threatened with a weapon were eighth grade students (19 percent), while at the same time this group was often threatened without a weapon (31 percent). Eighth grade students were tied with twelfth graders for students who reported property stolen (44 percent); eighth graders reported more of their property vandalized (34 percent) than any other grade group (National Center for Education Statistics, 1993).

Of eighth graders threatened with weapons in 1991, 27 percent were black and 22 percent were Hispanic. Of those actually injured with a weapon, 15 percent were black and 16 percent were Hispanic. During this same year, the majority of teachers who were threatened with injury (15 percent) and actually assaulted (15 percent) taught in urban schools (National Center for Education Statistics, 1993).

In contrast, a survey by Louis Harris and Associates of New York (Harris, 1993) found that most public school teachers (77 percent) felt safe when they were in or around school. Students felt less safe than teachers; 50 percent of students felt "very safe," and 40 percent felt only "somewhat safe." Among teachers and students, only a small number believed violence had increased in the past year, although a substantial proportion of students reported witnessing violent incidents either in or around school very often (6 percent) or sometimes (31 percent).

In this same study, teachers, students, and law enforcement officials agreed that most violent incidents occurred outside of school buildings. Most teachers and police officials believed that the major factors contributing to violence in public schools included lack of supervision at home, lack of family involvement in the schools, and exposure to violence in the mass media. Students cited more factors that contributed to violence, most relating to peer relations. Twenty-two percent of the students reported that their parents gave hardly any time or no time at all to a discussion of school life and homework (Harris, 1993).

Schools are microcosms of the larger society. Drugs, crime, and violence found in local communities are brought into the schools. Children having problems with dysfunctional families and who become filled with anger at or alienation from their parents are likely to act out in the classroom. The problems of the outside world are causing disorder in the traditionally protected environment of schools (Shepherd & Ragan, 1993).

An examination of arrest statistics is not sufficient to reveal the prevalence or seriousness of delinquency. Prevalence might be overestimated if, as some contend, a minority of repeat offenders is responsible for a highly disproportionate share of juvenile offenses. On the other hand, statistics may underestimate the problem because, as others point out, most offenses never come to police attention, and of those that do, few lead to arrests. Even data on gender, class, and ethnic differences in arrests are open to question. Boys are four times as likely to be arrested as girls, lower socioeconomic status adolescents are almost twice as likely to be arrested as middle-class adolescents, and African American and Latino youth are close to twice as likely to be arrested as European Americans.

It has been consistently shown that, at least in some jurisdictions, the police are more inclined to arrest lower socioeconomic status or dark-skinned teenagers than middle-class or light-skinned ones; the police may be similarly more inclined to arrest boys than girls. Moreover, arrest statistics are subject to marked variation in place and time, probably more because of the changing politics and policies of law enforcement than because of any changes in adolescent behavior (Berger, 1994).

The school-related misbehaviors studied most in recent years are violence, vandalism, and theft. Violence against teachers and other pupils, and the fear it produces, has increased at an alarming rate. During 1992, approximately 8 percent of urban junior and senior high school students missed at least one day of school each month because they were afraid to attend. About 282,000 students were physically attacked in U.S. secondary schools each month, and about 125,000 secondary school teachers (12 percent) were threatened with physical harm, with approximately 5,200 physically attacked (National Association of School Psychologists, 1993).

The tragedy of teacher assaults extends beyond the personal suffering of any teacher because such assaults destroy the trust upon which the student-teacher relationship rests. Once this trust is lost, teachers cannot teach effectively (Berger, 1994).

A major type of school disturbance that often goes unreported is sexual harassment by peers (Crews, Montgomery, & Garris, 1996). In junior high and high schools, girls and boys are sexually grabbed, called sexual names, embarrassed by jokes, and forced to perform sexual acts. Often this occurs in front of adults who fail to react. This harassment often results in girls doing poorly in their school work, having lower self-esteem, being depressed, and leaving class or school. In 1993, 94 percent of the incidents took place in the classroom and 76 percent in the hallway. Eighty-five percent of the girls and 76 percent of the boys reported that they had been subjected to unwanted sexual attention that interfered with their lives. Youth become mistrustful of adults who fail to intervene, provide equal protection, or otherwise safeguard the educational environment (Safe Schools Coalition, 1994).

Bullying is another major problem facing students in schools. Research indicates that male bullies are three to four times more likely to inflict physical assault than girls. Girls tend to be more subtle and psychologically manipulative. As with alcoholism and other forms of abusive behavior, evidence strongly suggests that bullying tends to be an intergenerational problem. Many childhood bullies are often abused at home by a parent or witness parents abuse each other and their siblings. Research has indicated that parents of bullies tend to ignore their children and do not really know what is happening to them.

Contrary to popular belief, bullying victims are not always different from other adolescents. Victims are often overprotected by parents who encourage dependent behavior. Bullying affects school attendance and the overall campus climate because victims fear school itself as well as the abuse that awaits them. Victims are also far more likely than other students to bring a weapon to school to protect themselves (Office of Juvenile Justice and Delinquency Prevention, 1991).

About one of every seven children is either a bully or a victim of a bully, and approximately 282,000 students are physically attacked in U.S. secondary schools each month. In an average month, about 125,000 secondary school teachers (12 percent) are threatened with physical harm, and 5,200 are physically attacked (National Association of School Psychologists, 1993).

There are some central trends in juvenile delinquency in the United States. Juveniles commit nearly twice their share (given their percentage of the population) of the nation's violent crimes. Between 1983 and 1992, juvenile arrest rates for murder rose 128 percent. The number of children arrested for illegally carrying or possessing weapons increased 66 percent between 1988 and 1992. Relatively few children are responsible for the bulk of serious, violent juvenile crime. Children are the prime targets of this juvenile crime, with guns exacerbating the problem (*National Center for Education Statistics*, 1994).

Schools now practice a different kind of safety drill: To their tornado, fire, and earthquake drills, many schools have added yellow-code (warning) alert and gunfire drills to their safety plans. Students are taught to dive under their desks when they hear gunfire or at the sound of a warning alarm (National Center for Educational Statistics, 1992).

The Schools and Staffing Survey, conducted by the National Center for Education Statistics (1992) in 1987–88 and 1990–91, asked teachers and principals their views of the problems in their schools. When asked about a range of school problems including absenteeism, student drug abuse, and physical conflicts among students, teachers and principals could respond that each problem was a serious problem, moderate problem, minor problem, or not a problem in their schools. It would be expected that with the current media coverage on school violence and other disturbances, drug abuse and conflicts would receive a rating of "serious," but that has not been the case.

In 1990–91, one of every four public school teachers cited lack of parent involvement as a serious problem in their schools (20.6 percent elementary and 30.7 percent secondary school teachers). The school problems viewed as serious by at least 10 percent of public school teachers included poverty, student disrespect for teachers, student tardiness (18.9 percent for elementary and 15.2 percent for secondary school teachers); parental alcoholism (11.6 percent for elementary and 12.5 percent secondary school teachers) or other drug abuse; student apathy (10.4 percent elementary and 31.7 percent secondary school teachers); and student absenteeism (6.1 percent elementary and 22.9 percent for secondary teachers) (National Center for Education Statistics, 1992).

Ironically, in 1991, fewer secondary school teachers viewed alcohol and drug abuse by students as serious problems in their schools than in 1988. Despite recent increasing attention to the presence of guns and other weapons on school grounds, fewer teachers reported student possession of weapons as a serious problem in 1991 than they did in 1988. Very few public school principals reported student possession of weapons as a serious problem in their schools. Only 0.5 percent of public secondary school principals said that this was a serious problem in 1988 and 1991 (Harris, 1993). The following is a brief table of these results.

	Percent Rated Serious By:			
	School Teachers		School Principals	
Problem	1988	1991	1988	1991
Alcohol use	21.5	16.1	11.7	7.1
Drug abuse	14.9	8.2	5.4	2.6
Weapons possession	2.6	2.2	0.3	0.5

These statistics actually show a decrease in severity rating by teachers and principals instead of an increase, as is often reported by media.

POSSIBLE CAUSES OF SCHOOL DISTURBANCE IN THE UNITED STATES

Traditional Theories

Traditional theories of why youth become delinquent range from the concept of free will (the belief that all humans are rational and make decisions by weighing the pros and cons and by seeking pleasure over pain) to the hard deterministic view (the belief that some individuals should not be held accountable for their actions because of mental feebleness or biological factors). In between these two schools of thought lies the soft deterministic view (the view that society affects behavior and influences how children view their world and react to it) (Drowns & Hess, 1990).

The classical (free will) school of thought, developed by Cesare Beccaria (1738–94), described people as free agents, pursuing hedonistic aims, and able to decide rationally on all or most courses of action. Offenders were viewed as possessing free will and being no different from nonoffenders except that they willed to commit crimes. It followed, naturally, that punishment was expected to be harsh and immediate so that offenders would "unwill" to commit future crimes. The offenders' mental makeups, backgrounds, and extenuating circumstances were irrelevant (Vold, 1968).

The positivism school of thought, founded by Cesare Lombroso (1835–1909), emphasized the criminal offender's personal and background characteristics rather than just the rational thought process and free will. The positivism school rejected the classical school's beliefs that people exercise reason and are capable of choice and free will and that offenders are no different from nonoffenders. Lombroso felt that offenders were sick and that their behaviors merely reflected the various determinants in their backgrounds: the biological, psychological, sociological, cultural, and physical environments. Correcting deviant behavior would require treatment of these determinants (Matza, 1964).

Under this heading of environmental impact lie several different groups of theories to explain juvenile delinquency. The first, the sociological theory, suggests that society conditions people to act in certain ways and that socialization will cause or prevent criminal behavior.

One such theory is the social structure and anomie theory by Robert Merton. Merton built on the work of Emile Durkheim, which focused on the idea of anomie: when individuals feel disconnected from any group and isolated from the mainstream of interaction and positive peer support. Merton noted that three conditions determine whether someone will become a criminal: the goals or aspirations that people learn from their cultures, the norms that people employ when attempting to achieve the goals, and the institutionalized means that are available for goal achievement (Merton, 1938).

A second sociological theory is Frederick Thrasher's gang theory, which describes how gangs often originate naturally from spontaneous play groups. The major factor that transforms a play group into a gang is conflict with other groups. As a result of that conflict, it becomes mutually beneficial for individuals to band together in the form of a gang to protect their rights and to satisfy needs that are not satisfied by environment and family. By middle adolescence, the gang has distinctive characteristics: a name, a mode of operation, and usually an ethnic or racial emphasis (Thrasher, 1936).

Behavioral theorists believe that people act in certain ways because their lifestyle behaviors are taught, not fixed. A well-known behavioral theory is Edwin Sutherland's differential association theory, which states that criminal behavior is learned in interaction with other persons. Most of the learning of criminal behavior occurs within intimate personal groups. When criminal behavior is learned, the learning includes not only techniques for committing the crime but also a specific direction for motives, drives, rationalizations, and attitudes (Cohen, Lindesmith, & Schuessler, 1956).

Biological theories concentrate on the belief that criminal behavior is inbred, not learned. Some psychological approaches state that criminal behaviors develop from emotional problems and disturbed personalities. Biochemical research demonstrates how diet, sweets, allergies, and blood chemistry can affect behavior. Neurological dysfunctions may cause learning disabilities and low intelligence quotient (IQ) scores, which shape at-risk personality types that are very susceptible to criminal behavior (Drowns & Hess, 1990).

Much concern remains over the cause of rampant violence in U.S. schools. Many believe that the root cause is the number of weapons on U.S. streets, that guns are replacing the "sticks and stones will break my bones" of the childhood adage and therefore contribute to school violence; increasingly, many believe that this is why teachers are in more danger in the 1990s than they were 5, 10, or 20 years ago. Others believe that the causes of rampant school violence are gangs and drugs in the schools: Gangs are intimidating their classmates and thus contributing to the growth of school violence. Still others believe that the cause is connected to fighting words, with girls and boys more inclined to speak their minds in the 1990s, thus causing more conflict (Wooden, 1995).

The majority hold the opinion that the primary cause of school disturbance is the growing lack of parental concern: They believe that parents are less caring than they were years ago (Wooden, 1995).

One reason U.S. students seem to be lagging in educational achievement is that many do not read in or out of school. In 1990, a government survey found that 45 percent of fourth graders, 63 percent of eighth graders, and 59 percent of twelfth graders read a total of ten or fewer pages each day. Fewer than half of all students read outside of school, about 30 percent reported never reading for fun, and about 22 percent said either they did not have homework assigned or they simply did not do it. About 5 percent of the students surveyed reported having fewer than 25 books in their home, and 15 percent to 25 percent said they did not subscribe to magazines or newspapers. Another suspected culprit is excessive television viewing: 62 percent of fourth graders, 64 percent of eighth graders, and 40 percent of twelfth graders report watching at least three hours of television each day; about 25 percent of the fourth graders watch six hours or more per day (Owen, 1991).

Adolescent Views

Obviously, there are many different beliefs about why youth become deviant. Many of the research-based variables center on the issues of boredom and alienation. Some delinquents are actually hyperactive and need extra stimulation to keep them interested; they may become deviant because of the desire for risk and excitement. Youth may see themselves as being forced into becoming good citizens by society and their parents; freedom for them is testing the limit and getting away with their possibly unacceptable behavior. Some youth become trapped in this behavior because of an unhappiness with self or with the outside world: Committing crime may be one way to find something at which they are competent. Some delinquent behavior of middle- or upper-class youth evolves more from parental abuse, indifference, and neglect than from economic hardship (Wooden, 1995).

Much of the current problem of negative student views may be caused by lack of communication. Few students talk to teachers about their personal problems or problems at home (22 percent) or about where they can get help with personal or family problems (13 percent). Most students do not talk to teachers about problems they may be having with their peers. Students do not discuss their personal problems with teachers for a wide variety of reasons: because they believe there is no privacy or confidentiality in school (26 percent), because they feel adults do not understand them (22 percent), because they think teachers cannot help (20 percent), and because teachers do not seem interested in, or do not have time for, their students (24 percent) (Harris, 1995).

Although adults commit most of the crime in the United States, teenagers are inspiring more of the current fear. A recent CNN Gallup Poll (1994) suggested that juveniles lead the list of people perceived as would-be criminals. When asked what type of person would most likely victimize another, 58 percent of those surveyed reported male teenagers. Seventy-one percent of respondents from inner-city areas felt the same way.

Psychological Factors

Many psychological factors contribute to the problems of youth. Those who become delinquent are more likely to be socially assertive, suspicious, defiant, destructive, ambivalent to authority, impulsive, resentful, lacking self-control, and hostile (Drowns & Hess, 1990).

The developmental period of adolescence is probably the most well-researched correlate of juvenile delinquency. Adolescence brings biological, psychological, emotional, and social stress. Adolescents pretend to be adults by doing what they think adults do: dress like adults, talk like adults, smoke, have sex, and drink alcohol (Drowns & Hess, 1990).

Acting out is a behavior related to the developmental stage of adolescence. Traditionally there has been one comprehensive definition of acting out: the free, deliberate, often malicious indulgence of impulses, which frequently leads to aggression as well as other manifestations of delinquency such as vandalism, cruelty to animals, and even murder.

There is a desire for immediate gratification and an absence of self-control (Drowns & Hess, 1990).

This acting out may result from an early history of severe parental reaction or deprivation or from witnessing or experiencing physical abuse and violence. Adolescents may strike out to hurt the world they see as hostile and to gain a sense of importance by overcoming feelings of inferiority. This phenomenon can be found in all socioeconomic levels of society (Drowns & Hess, 1990).

Vulnerability to peer pressure peaks in early adolescence, usually between sixth and ninth grades, and often leads to conflicts with parents; adolescents report the greatest number of disagreements in the ninth grade. There is also a decline in self-esteem, particularly among girls. At a time when adolescents are seeking stronger peer associations and supportive climates for resolving identity issues, they are confronted with an educational environment that is more impersonal (Elkind, 1984).

Most acting out occurs when adolescents are moving from elementary school to middle school to high school, where many students are strangers to each other and new relationships must be formed. In addition, the peer group does not remain constant during the day, which makes relationship establishment even more difficult. This is an anxiety-provoking situation: Adolescents fear not knowing anyone. By conforming to the norms of peer groups and becoming accepted, young adolescents meet many of their socioemotional needs — especially the need for affiliation. Parenting styles may also be responsible for tendencies to seek out the peer group. For example, when parents maintain restrictiveness and limit opportunities for decision making, their children tend to turn to the peer group for advice and support. In addition, transition in schools frequently coincides with other life changes such as the onset of puberty, dating, family disruptions (such as divorce), or a move to a new neighborhood (Garrin & Furman, 1989).

Whenever, at any age, children are confronted with transitions, they adjust best if they have emotional and social supports to cope with the demands. Students with strong relationships with peers and teachers show higher academic performance, less anxiety, and more favorable attitudes toward school. Thus, these students are less likely to commit acts of violence or to drop out of school (Garrin & Furman, 1989).

Although many adolescents have the cognitive competence to think logically, they often fail to do so, especially when thinking about themselves. They have difficulty thinking logically about immediate experiences; their thoughts tend to be flawed by adolescent egocentrism (Garrin & Furman, 1989).

As part of egocentrism, adolescents often create imaginary audiences for themselves as they fantasize how others will react to their appearance and behavior. They assume everyone notices and judges their appearance and skills. An imaginary audience tends to be composed of peers rather than adults. When adolescents become more comfortable and secure in their social world, they become more secure, more realistic, and more positive, and they rely on their own opinions and beliefs rather than those of an audience. Girls are generally more concerned than boys about the imaginary audience, and younger teens are more concerned than older teens; however, delinquent boys think more about imagined opinions than do nondelinquents of either sex (Elkind, 1984).

Adolescent thought processes are characterized by the abilities to imagine possibilities and to deny reality when it interferes with adolescent fantasy. A result of this fantasy is the personal fable, one aspect of which is the invincibility myth. Many adolescents feel immune to laws of probability and mortality; they engage in risk taking, secure in the belief that they will not be killed, become sick or pregnant, or get hurt or caught. They also tend to see themselves as destined for greatness. These adolescents imagine their lives as heroic, see themselves as destined for wealth and greatness, and may have already decided that school is a waste of their time. This aspect of the personal fable is influenced by what is deemed as valuable in one's peer culture (Elkind, 1984).

By late adolescence or early adulthood, young people become better able to reason logically. Consequently, they become more secure and more realistic. As a result, delinquent behavior decreases because of cognitive maturity rather than punitive measures (Elkind, 1984).

Chronic Delinquency

Following is a typical profile of a delinquent: a male who has abused drugs (75 percent), committed at least 50 felonies, is impulsive, began crime at an early age (five or six), and shuns responsibility. His behavior has caused his family to give up on him. He is unwilling to think, will skip school, and is prone to drop out. His friends will typically have the same profile (Drowns & Hess, 1990).

Two noteworthy aspects of chronic juvenile delinquency are that most chronic juvenile offenders start their criminal careers before age 12 and tend to come from poorer, inner-city, disorganized neighborhoods. It is hypothesized that there are three pathways to chronic delinquency: overt — from aggression, to fighting, to violence; covert — from minor covert behavior, to property damage, to serious delinquency; and authority conflict — from stubborn behavior, to defiance, to authority avoidance. It is believed that these chronic offenders commit 75 percent of the juvenile crime in any given year (*Office of Juvenile Justice and Delinquency Prevention*, 1994).

Other characteristics of chronic violent juvenile offenders include being less attached to and less monitored by their parents, more likely residing in poor high-crime areas, having less commitment to school and attachment to teachers, having more delinquent peers, being more apt to belong to gangs, and acting out in school (*Office of Juvenile Justice and Delinquency Prevention*, 1994).

Psychopathic or sociopathic behavior is another factor that may contribute to school disturbance and violence. These concepts refer to chronic asocial behavior rooted in severe deficiencies in the development of a socially appropriate conscience. To differentiate: whereas psychopaths do not know the difference between right or wrong, sociopaths know the difference between right or wrong but do not care. There is a lack of guilt feelings appropriate to society. These adolescents often lack role models, parental control, or parents with social values (Drowns & Hess, 1990).

Antisocial and At-risk Youth

The decade of the 1990s is seeing a greater development of antisocial youth who expect school to serve their purposes, choose not to apply themselves, and perceive school as a place to socialize. For antisocial youth, the use of drugs is often a shortcut to obtain money, to generate excitement, or to escape reality; they are constantly seeking the easy way to go, digging into one hole after another, and not heeding warnings. Often, the only time they seek other lifestyles is after severe personal tragedies. The measured intelligence levels of these individuals are low; many cannot read or write. Many antisocial youth are thought to have learning disabilities, but most are illiterate because they will not take the time to learn (Drowns & Hess, 1990).

The 1990s have also seen the development of what is often called a generation of at-risk students. Donmoyer and Kos (1993) conclude that there are sufficient commonalities in U.S. culture and enough similarities among classrooms, schools, and districts within that culture so that some students will more than likely be categorized as at risk in any educational setting. These students either display clearly identifiable physical, cognitive, or emotional conditions or have background and family circumstances that severely hamper their ability to learn in any of this culture's classrooms and schools. Special assistance will be required to help these students as well as other students whose problems are masked by their ability to play the school's social game, even while they are failing to master essential academic material. Also, large numbers of students who are classified as being at risk in certain educational situations would be quite successful if classroom and school characteristics changed. This fact encourages many observers to move beyond an epidemiological perspective and its attempts to identify personal characteristics and conditions that predispose students to being at risk. Instead, educators must focus on the properties of schools and classrooms that encourage success and failure. Educators can more easily control school and classroom variables than they can the personal, socioeconomically based variables traditionally associated with the term at risk (Donmoyer & Kos, 1993).

Group Membership

Delinquency often originates from the group membership acquired by a child. Sometimes a child's membership in a certain group is not of his or her choosing. Instead, perceptions or stereotyping by others will label that child as a member. One of the earliest theories of juvenile delinquency causation involved the concept of labeling. Edwin Lemert is usually believed to be the most important contributor to the delinquency labeling approach. The deviant label is attached, and the juvenile becomes stigmatized, having little opportunity to be rewarded for good behavior. This label then becomes a self-fulfilling prophecy. The primary deviance is the original act, and the secondary deviance most often results from the labeling (Drowns & Hess, 1990).

Groups such as punk rockers feel alienated from what they perceive as the complacency and mindless conformity of their peers. Groups such as racist skinheads are motivated by the changes in racial diversity taking place and disapprove of accepting minorities. Most of these youth will eventually outgrow defiance and become independent thinkers, but some do not (Wooden, 1995).

School itself often becomes an environment in which separatist grouping occurs. Groupings in segments of prejudice are often known as cliques. The following is an example of the clique structure (based on popularity) that can be found in a typical U.S. high school:

1. Jocks — boys who participate in sports
2. Cheerleaders — attractive, school spirited

3. Tweakies — boys who have an extremely "laid back" attitude

4. Trendies/socs/preppies — desperate to fit in and spend much time shopping

5. Drama freaks — students who are completely engrossed in acting

6. Bandos — students who are completely engrossed in band

7. Smacks/brains — students who have an extremely high GPA

8. Dirtbags — middle-class but considered "low-lifes" by others

9. Sluts —girls who wear provocative clothing

10. Punks — dress in torn jeans, combat boots, and mohawks

11. Death rockers/metal heads — live and act like the music

12. Loners — no peer group with whom to socialize, always alone

(Wooden, 1995, p. 51)

Impact of School

The U.S. educational system as a whole may be a cause of school violence. Budget cuts have severely reduced education resources in many communities and have curtailed state support for local school systems. Spending on U.S. elementary and secondary education trails that of other nations. While Sweden spends 7 percent of its gross national product on education, Austria 6 percent, and Japan 4.8 percent, the United States spends 4.1 percent. As a consequence, the United States does not provide the classroom services routinely available to children in other nations (Sivard, 1989).

Many educators believe that part of the violence facing schools is caused by the schools themselves. Albert Einstein was quoted as follows: "The worst thing seems to be for schools to work with methods of fear, force, and artificial authority. Such treatment destroys the healthy feelings, the integrity, and the self-confidence of pupils" (Curcio & First, 1993).

According to many educators, allowing corporal punishment of children by school officials results in violent actions directed toward students. Each year, more than 1 million incidents of corporal punishment occur in U.S. schools, with 10,000 requiring medical attention. Some educators believe that all use of corporal punishment teaches children to use force when trying to control another's behavior. Children come to believe that force is a way to solve conflicts and that the physically larger person will control any given situation; school administrators who allow corporal punishment should not be surprised, therefore, when students act out and become violent — it is what the students have been taught (Curcio & First, 1993).

R. M. Regoli and J. D. Hewitt (1994) described four traditional school-based influences on student delinquent behavior at school. The first is loss of teacher authority. Teachers must maintain their authority and need a strong principal to stand behind them. When principals and parents do not support teachers, children will not support teachers. After authority is lost, control of students is lost.

The second influence on delinquent behavior is regimentation and revenge. As students age, they are given much more independence and control — but often not in school. School rules often do not grow with the students. Faced with strict rules and degrading experiences in class, some students try to save face and regain their self-esteem by lashing out at the perceived cause of their embarrassment. Teachers then become victims of attack, and school property the objects of vandalism (Regoli & Hewitt, 1994).

Tracking students is the third school-based influence on delinquency. Placing students in a college track, technical track, or vocational track frequently causes problems. Placement is dictated often by appearance and socioeconomic status rather than by ability. Low-track students tend to receive lower grades than other students, even for work of equal quality, on the basis that students who are not college bound are less bright and do not need the good grades to get into college. Teachers of high-ability students make more of an effort to teach in an interesting and challenging manner than those who instruct lower-level students (New Jersey Juvenile Delinquency Commission, 1972).

Tracking frequently involves the concept of the self-fulfilling prophecy. Students from whom little achievement and much misbehavior are expected tend to live up to these often unspoken assumptions about them. Placement into a low track leads to loss of self-esteem and increases the potential for academic failure and disturbances, both in and out of school. Students segregated in lower tracks develop value systems that often reward misbehavior in lieu of the academic success that eludes them. Lower-track students are less inclined to conform. Because they see no future rewards of their schooling, these students do not realize their futures can be threatened by a record of deviant behavior or low academic achievement.

IQ and Delinquency

The fourth school-based influence on delinquency cited by Regoli and Hewitt is IQ testing. IQ and delinquency seem to be strongly related (Regoli & Hewitt, 1994).

Early criminologists who trained in medicine or psychology and who used intelligence tests made some inflated and, in some cases, ridiculous claims about the relationship between intelligence and crime. These criminologists suggested that people of low intelligence were easily led into law breaking by more clever people and that they failed to realize committing an offense in a certain way often led to getting caught and being punished (Slawson, 1926).

Contemporary research consistently finds a relationship between IQ and delinquency. T. Hirschi and M. Hindelang (1977) reported the average delinquent has an IQ about eight points lower than law-abiding juveniles. They also reported that IQ was associated with the type of crime likely to be committed. Bribers, embezzlers, and forgers score higher than auto thieves, burglars, and substance-abuse offenders who, in turn, score higher than those who commit assault, murder, and rape.

Theories of delinquency generally ignore these findings, and exactly how IQ affects delinquency remains a mystery. One possibility is that IQ has no effect. It may be that both IQ and delinquency are caused by some third variable such as social class (Chambliss & Ryther, 1975). A second possibility is that low IQs do not lead to higher rates of delinquency per se but merely to higher rates of apprehension (Haskell & Yablonsky, 1978).

A third possibility is that IQ directly affects delinquency. J. Q. Wilson and R. Herrnstein (1985) believe that adolescents with low intelligence may be more impulsive or lacking in moral reasoning. They argue that people with low intelligence will favor impulsive crimes with immediate rewards and those with high intelligence, the inverse.

Hirschi (1969) suggests a fourth possibility: that IQ affects delinquency indirectly. The effect of IQ is transmitted through school-experience variables. The original purpose of IQ tests was to predict how well a person would do in school and, although they are not perfect, IQ tests have a reasonably good prediction record: Students who perform well on IQ tests tend to get good grades.

Impact of Family

There are two traditional approaches to the study of parental impact on children's behavior. First is the genetic heredity approach, which holds that genetic vulnerability is passed on to children. It is very difficult to separate the effects of heredity from environment when families live in similar social situations and often in the same homes or communities from one generation to the next. Parent and child may be affected by similar conditions of poverty, levels of neighborhood violence, and negative social interactions (Walters & White, 1989).

Second, and often more popular, is the social approach theory, which emphasizes the modeling of behavior for the child. In this approach the antisocial trait in parents is related to their disciplinary practices, which, in turn, result in the child's antisocial behavior. In effect, the parents establish antisocial norms in the home, which can be done most often by antisocial talk. A culture of deviance is established through the telling of war stories to or in front of children, and the behavior is modeled (Drowns & Hess, 1990).

A. Bandura and R. H. Walters (1963) developed the concept of modeling: Children copy the behavior of people whom they hold in high esteem and who have provided rewards. These models are typically the children's parents. Models can also be siblings, peers, athletes, and television personalities.

The impact of family relations on children can never be overstated. Family is a significant force in the growth of a child. The structure and patterns of interaction at home influence prosocial and antisocial behavior. The family can have positive impacts by insulating children from antisocial behavior, controlling criminal behavior, controlling rewards, and maintaining positive relationships. Delinquency is highest when positive family interaction and control are weak and conflict is high. Family is seen as an immediate origin of delinquency — family structure through childhood influences how strong peer pressure can be for a child, and family influences affect the possible attractiveness of negative groups (Drowns & Hess, 1990).

Divorce is one of the strongest emotional events that can influence the family. The absence of one parent, the emotional and financial tension, and sometimes the continuing conflicts between parents that accompany divorce frequently lead to psychological problems for children. The worst period for a child is the first year of divorce, when aggression, distractibility and noncompliance, academic difficulties, poor relationships with peers, and low self-esteem emerge. These negative effects are most apparent in boys, and generally diminish with time (two to three years). Using a longitudinal design, however, some studies found many boys still exhibiting the patterns described above at six years after divorce. Adaptation seems to depend on parenting style and conflict following the divorce.

Generally, children who are strongly attached to both parents have a lower probability of self-reported delinquency than children who are strongly attached to only one parent. Furthermore, children living in single-parent homes who are strongly attached to the custodial parent generally have a greater probability of committing delinquent acts than children living in intact homes who are strongly attached to both parents (Garrin & Furman, 1989).

The family is considered the first teacher, first role model, first social institution, and first classroom. If parent and child do not communicate well, appropriate behavior may not be learned. Family life establishes a sense of right and wrong. Within the family, children learn attitudes and values that they keep throughout life (Drowns & Hess, 1990).

Another major area of concern is socialization outside the family. Children must learn respect for others, social and moral values, suppression of behavior considered undesirable, honesty and fair play, and conformity to social values. A family can ideally reinforce all of these and rush to correct violations (Drowns & Hess, 1990).

C. R. Shaw and H. McKay (1969) theorized that disorganization in society and disorganization within the home can have the greatest impact on delinquent behavior. They felt that economic status has a great deal to do with the rates of delinquent behavior: The greater the economic deprivation, the greater the delinquency; and the less the economic deprivation, the less the delinquency. It is believed that persons living in disadvantaged environments often have the same material aspirations as persons living in advantaged environments; however, residents in disadvantaged areas soon learn that gaining legitimate access to their goals is difficult. The disparity between their goals and the means available for legitimately achieving them creates a situation conducive to deviancy, delinquency, and crime in urban areas.

Homes of delinquent youth are typically disorganized: There are no set routines for family activity and no protective shield for the children, parents ignore them, and family policies are inconsistent. Dysfunctional homes can also result in runaways. Adolescents resort to running away when they feel they can cope only by leaving; they may feel the entire world is against them, and there is no other choice but to leave. More problems occur after adolescents have run away and become streetwise, use drugs, or become involved in crime, prostitution, and other illegal activities. Adolescents report reasons for leaving home as conflict with parents, alienation, rejection, hostile control, lack of warmth, lack of affection, and lack of parental support. If leaving does not work, adolescents often turn to suicide. Suicidal persons see themselves as unable to cope because the environment is against them; they see themselves as alone and at the mercy of a hostile world (Drowns & Hess, 1990).

A relatively new area of research examines the concept of victimization of children (that is, victim of personal harm or theft). Major variables that predict victimization of children are gender, number of siblings, exposure to violence outside school, and personal violence-related attributes. Across the country, only about one in ten victimizations appears random (not predicted by the aforementioned variables). Often the violence is brought in from outside the school rather than being generated by the school. Victimized students share characteristics that put them at higher risk of gun-related victimization than other students. Given the large number of victimizations and the large number of respondents at risk, intervention at the individual level would be ineffective. Alteration of community social structure and culture is the appropriate means to reduce gun-related victimization levels (Sheley, McGee, & Wright, 1992).

Many parents feel that major signs of juvenile delinquency are adolescent fads such as outlandish dress and permanent physical changes such as body piercing, tattoos, or branding. Although students see these changes as attention-getting devices, parents sometimes believe that the students are sending visual messages to peers, teachers, and other adults that they have no respect for anyone or anything. Many psychologists believe that these changes are simply providing ways for teenagers to express their individuality and assert their independence. Psychologists also warn that parents must be cautious about letting these fashion trends lead to major family battles. A positive approach is talking to teenagers and helping them consider all of the consequences of their actions before making permanent changes to their bodies. For nonpermanent changes, most psychologists believe that adolescent fads will change with the times and have no lasting effects (Drowns & Hess, 1990).

A root problem for much of the country is the very high poverty rate, especially among children and among those who live in rural areas. Living in acute poverty is correlated with malnutrition, psychopathology, and lack of growth (Drowns & Hess, 1990). Large numbers of children are born at risk of dying as infants, are being raised by teenage mothers or unmarried mothers, and are susceptible to drugs, crime, and unemployment. Test results and other evaluative instruments reveal that the United States is producing a poorly educated adult population lacking any capacity as a good role model and is saddled with a job structure that provides for a large number of low-pay, low-skill jobs (Hodgkinson, 1990).

Children who grow up in poverty or without adequate supervision at home are at risk for later criminality. Drugs accelerate a juvenile's crime rate, while negative peer influences can cause a shift to criminality. Children who do poorly in school or who drop out are among the more likely to become criminals (Regoli & Hewitt, 1994).

The concept of environmental impact on behavior is not a new one. Research on the impact of the environment dates back to a study first conducted by Clifford R. Shaw (Regoli & Hewitt, 1994) in his examination of the ecological theory of crime, which concerns the areas where crime and delinquency seem most likely to occur. Shaw studied crime and delinquency statistics recorded in Chicago between 1900 and 1927. More than 55,000 juvenile delinquents and some criminals were found to live in certain zones of the city. Shaw concluded that many of the law violations recorded were acceptable behaviors within the specific settings in which the offenders lived. Shaw also concluded that most other theories of crime causation must be viewed in the context of an individual's environment.

SUMMARY

In any historical examination of school disturbance and juvenile delinquency, two concepts become immediately apparent. First, juvenile delinquency has existed for as long as juveniles have existed. Second, school disturbance and violence have existed for as long as schools have existed. Many feel that these are two social issues that have only recently become serious problems and areas of concern in the United States. In actuality, problems with juvenile misbehavior and problems in passing along knowledge from teacher to student have plagued societies around the world and throughout recorded history. The history of the United States is no different.

National statistical reports and surveys have revealed a stabilization and significant decrease in almost all areas of reported crime over the past two decades. These same reports also show that during this time, youth violence and random violence have drastically increased. These opposing trends have had an interesting impact on public perception. The trend in increased youth violence has not allowed the U.S. public to derive much comfort from the trend in crime stabilization. People are still afraid in their neighborhhoods and cities, and more so in their schools.

The answer to the question of how much school disturbance and juvenile delinquency exists in the United States often depends on what source is sought for an answer. Juvenile justice department records offer the answer that in the past ten years, juvenile involvement in violent crime has increased by 62 percent to 85 percent (Office of Juvenile Justice and Delinquency Prevention, 1991a). National surveys continue to suggest that the answer is that hundreds of thousands of weapons are brought to schools each day and that the same number of students are threatened daily by these weapons. On the other hand, surveys conducted by private agencies find that there is less violence occurring in schools than what the popular media is reporting. Surveys of teachers find that a very high percentage feel safe in their schools; surveys of students find that a very high percentage also feel safe in their schools.

Research reports offer information that sexual harassment and bullying have been found to be two new areas of school disturbance that are only now, in the 1990s, receiving the attention they deserve. The extent of illegal drug use and alcohol use is also debatable at any time. U.S. Department of Justice reports show that illegal drug use is experiencing a drastic increase in the 1990s; however, student self-report surveys and surveys of teachers show that use has actually continued to decrease since approximately 1982 and that parental involvement and other student issues are the actual cornerstone to many, if not all, of these problems.

Humans have sought to explain abnormal behavior since they became aware of their own existence. The earliest explanations were spiritual in nature: People (young and old) could become possessed by evil spirits and commanded to commit evil deeds. As human thought evolved, so did the capacity to explain the criminal element in society. This thinking has swung between two extremes: one that humans operate under total free will and make all decisions for self-benefit, the other that some members of society cannot control their behaviors because of biological factors. It has only been relatively recently that children were viewed as having special needs and being in special circumstances. For the vast majority of history, children were viewed the same as adults, treated the same as adults, and punished the same as adults.

The history of the United States and its education of its children is one that demonstrates how all of these influences throughout history have shaped U.S. society, U.S. education, and, therefore, U.S. school violence.

2

Colonial Period, 1600–1780

Education in the United States has always followed a course directed by the prominent social developments of the time. Chapter 1 began an examination of social and educational developments and their impacts on the evolution of school disturbance from the early colonial period to the mid-1990s. Chapter 2 discusses the major social and educational changes that occurred between 1600 and 1780. School disturbance in early America is discussed in light of social and educational philosophies and practices of the time.

SOCIAL DEVELOPMENTS

Some of the social concerns of the colonial period included the settlement of the first colonies, a chronic labor shortage, the Great Awakening, the printing press, and the Revolutionary War.

One major influence in early America was the concern immediately following the Revolutionary War when the issue of future U.S. leadership was undecided. Unlike England, where heredity and nobility were a source of leadership, the United States was left with a new government and no solid means of developing leaders. Benjamin Rush and George Washington each proposed a national university as a means of preparing political leaders and creating a common national culture. This idea, however, was never realized. Critics charged that a national university would result in elitism; the trained leaders would view themselves as better than the average citizen and therefore would not be able to represent the interests and welfare of the general public (Spring, 1989).

As an answer to the charge of elitism, the concept of meritocracy was introduced. This would involve a social system in which everyone would have an equal chance to develop his or her own talents and rise in the social hierarchy. In theory, this is the system present in the United States today (Spring, 1989). One result of the meritocracy ideal was Thomas Jefferson's *Bill for the More General Diffusion of Knowledge*, which will be discussed later in this chapter. Jefferson's proposal resulted in a very limited education for the general population. He did not feel it necessary for the populace to be well educated in order to be productive citizens. Instead he believed that natural reasoning would lead the individual in political decisions, and the political education of the citizens would come from the free press (Spring, 1989).

EDUCATIONAL DEVELOPMENTS

Colonial Education

In colonial America, schooling was unsystematic, unregulated, and discontinuous. Much of colonial education involved wide diversity in institution and method of support. In reference to public school, the term "public" had two connotations: It implied first that students were taught as a group rather than individually and second that the effort was an investment for public benefit. Public schooling in this era was a state-owned and -regulated system that was supported by community taxation, organized and officiated by community leaders, and in which children of a certain age were compelled to attend. This system can be contrasted with educational movements by private entities, which essentially did not exist in colonial America. Parents played a large role in the initiative for schooling, which was not neglected because of the rapid population growth throughout the colonial period. Common figures demonstrate that as much as 50 percent of the male population received some sort of formal education. This fact is surprising when one considers that, except for the ministry, occupational training and advancement were not linked to schooling. Education in colonial America served the primary purposes of moral and social training (Carper, 1995).

Sources of Education

Colonial education consisted of a four-pronged structure: family, church, school, and press. Family in the New World was important because parents, whose time was spent building a life in the savage wilderness, were afraid that children, if not attended, would resort to a savagery similar to that found in the frontier. Therefore, colonial parents were forced to rely on school and schoolteachers much more than did their European counterparts. Such fear led to the 1642 Compulsory Education Law in the Massachusetts Bay Colony, which held parents legally responsible for educating their children (Perkinson, 1995). The law mandated that masters and parents instruct children in religion, reading, and capital laws, and it was enforced by the colony selectmen (Carper, 1995). A problem, however, arose with this new compulsory education. Parents needed little encouragement to educate their children, but few had time left in their busy days after securing the basic necessities of life. The result was the establishment of the 1647 school law commonly known as the "Old Deluder Satan" law, which required each town to provide schools and school masters (Perkinson, 1995). Specifically, communities that consisted of 50 or more households were required to provide instruction in reading and writing; communities that consisted of 100 or more households were required to provide grammar schools (Spring, 1994).

Colonial children were also educated within the household. Common household tutorial materials consisted of the Holy Bible, John Foxe's *Book of Martyrs* (1563), Lewis Bayly's *Practice of Piety* (1612), John Bunyan's *Pilgrim's Progress* (1678), and Michael Wigglesworth's *Day of Doom* (1662) (Carper, 1995). As evidenced by these titles, colonial education placed great emphasis on religious instruction. Puritan leader John Winthrop stated in 1630, "We must consider that we shall be a city upon a hill. The eyes of all people are upon us" (Spring, 1994, p. 6). It was the goal of the early colonists to create a good society, which to them meant a "well-ordered religious society that would win God's approval and be used as a model by the rest of the world" (p. 6).

Another form of household education was the apprenticeship. Children were commonly apprenticed to a master for seven years, during which time the master was responsible for teaching the apprentice to read and write. Chronic labor shortages in the colonies, however, often resulted in an early termination of the apprenticeship and led to the neglect of masters and parents in providing proper instruction. This was one of the problems that the compulsory education laws were designed to eliminate. In addition, it was primarily the children of the poor who were apprenticed, and the instruction they received was for the purpose of maintaining religious piety and conforming to the power of the existing authority (Spring, 1994).

The colonial church, as one could imagine, played a strong role in the education of colonial children. In seventeenth- and eighteenth-century New England, people were taught to read and write so that they could understand and obey the laws of God and the state. Much of this view was a development of the Protestant Reformation, which resulted in the instruction for piety and the development of the good society espoused by John Winthrop. Some historians view the early American schools as a direct result of the Protestant revolts in Europe. Members of the Massachusetts Bay Colony considered reading and writing to serve the primary purpose of allowing individuals to read the Bible and religious tracts. This ideology led directly to the establishment of the previously discussed Compulsory Education Laws. Given that these communities were governed by the church, the result of compulsory education laws was the establishment of church-supported schools (Spring, 1994).

The printing press had a great impact on the education of American colonists. According to Lawrence Cremin, "Both the Renaissance and the Reformation cast Every man, for the first time in history, in the role of student, and the printing press made that role for the first time possible" (Carper, 1995, p. 42). The printing press made mass education not only possible but also, eventually, necessary. The printing press allowed for reproductions of books that had previously been hand-copied onto parchment and stored in monasteries. Everyone, including children, had access to knowledge. Scholars were able to permanently preserve and retrieve the writings of the ancient Greeks and Romans as well as the early Christians and Jews. Although mass education was possible, many in the New World felt that there was no need for it. The general consensus held that the masses were laborers who had no use for education other than piety. Traditionally, only the clergy were literate, but after the emergence of the printing press some aristocracy began educating their sons in the liberal arts. The beneficiaries of the new technology, therefore, were not the masses but the children of the aristocracy (Perkinson, 1995).

Types of Schools and Instructional Materials

The two categories of schools in colonial New England were town and private venture. Two popular forms of town schools were petty and grammar schools. Instruction in petty schools, also known as reading-and-writing schools, was primarily religious and authoritarian. Hornbooks such as

The New England Primer were used as the primary educational materials. Hornbooks consisted of a piece of wood with the lesson carved into it; these carvings were then protected by a thin sheet of horn spread over the top. Usually these lessons simply consisted of a prayer or the alphabet. *The New England Primer* opened with the alphabet and a guide to spelling. The alphabet was taught using an alphabetic listing of religious and authoritarian statements:

A wise son makes a glad Father, but a foolish son is the heaviness of his Mother.

Better is little with the fear of the Lord, than great treasure and trouble therewith.

Come unto CHRIST all ye that labour and are heavy laden, and He will give you
     rest.

or:

In **A**dam's Fall, We Sinned all.

Thy Life to Mend, This **B**ook Attend.

The **C**at doth Play, And after flay.

Other parts of the primer included the Lord's Prayer, the Creed, the Ten Commandments, books of the Old and New Testament, and a list of numbers (Spring, 1994).

Another method of instruction in petty schools consisted of the catechism, which was a series of questions and answers that students would memorize and recite. The short catechism found in *The New England Primer* provided instruction in the basic ideology of the Protestant faith with questions such as, "What do the Scriptures principally teach?" to which the answer was, "The Scriptures principally teach, what Man's to believe concerning God, and what duty God requireth of Man." The catechism would take the students through a series of religious doctrines, ending with the meaning of the Lord's Prayer (Spring, 1994).

Petty schools taught primarily reading, with some emphasis on writing and ciphering. A popular form of the petty school was the dame school, which was often conducted in the kitchen or living room of the teacher's home. Instruction in petty schools became a prerequisite for admission to grammar school. Students in petty schools were not asked to analyze or interpret the materials they were being taught, but rather were taught to accept the official versions as correct (Spring, 1994).

Grammar schools were another form of town school, differing from petty schools in that instruction included subject matter that prepared students for college and leadership positions. Generally, only the sons of the elite were sent to grammar schools and on to college. The Hopkins Grammar school at New Haven in 1694 stated its goal as "[the education] of hopeful youth in the Latin tongue, and other learned languages so far as to prepare such youths for the college and public service of the country in church and commonwealth" (Spring, 1994, p. 10). This goal was typical of grammar schools of the period. Particularly important in the grammar schools was the emphasis on classical Greek and Roman works, the study of which was considered paramount in the development of civic character and preparation for leadership. This ideology of conferring status led to the grammar school as an instrument for improvement of the middle class. In addition, grammar schools posed a direct threat to the aristocracy because their mere existence suggested that one could be educated to rule. As discussed earlier, the "Old Deluder Satan" law of 1647 required the establishment of grammar schools in communities of 100 or more households. By the eighteenth century, 39 grammar schools existed in the New England colonies (Spring, 1994).

Typically, grammar schools provided a seven-year education, with a major emphasis on the study of Latin and lesser emphasis on Greek and Hebrew. In particular, Latin grammar, Latin conversation and composition, Latin readings, Greek and Hebrew grammar, and Greek literature were taught (Spring, 1994).

In addition to public town schools, private venture schools existed. The New England aristocracy separated itself from the middle class beginning with reading-and-writing schools. The aristocratic children attended private dame schools rather than the town schools, while the children of the poor attended town schools and worked in apprenticeships.

Schooling in the middle colonies differed from schooling in New England. Three types of schools dominated this area: church, entrepreneurial, and charity schools. Church schools fell under denominational control of churches such as the Dutch Reformed, Lutheran, Mennonite, Amish, Moravian, Quaker, Baptist, Episcopalian, Presbyterian, and Catholic. These schools were established with the intention of educating members of the respective congregations in the region and were occasionally opened to all children in a geographic area. For example, the William Penn Charter School was opened in 1689 by the Quakers and chartered in 1697 as a public grammar school (Carper, 1995). As L. A. Cremin stated, "All these churches and communities taught quite as vigorously as the established churches perhaps even more so, since their religious instruction was often merely one aspect of a larger effort to preserve an entire ethnic tradition in the face of English cultural domination" (Cremin, 1970, p. 164).

Entrepreneurial schools were predominately found in New York and Philadelphia. These schools were usually without connection to any other school and, therefore, often unsupervised. Entrepreneurial schools worked much like a business with a product to sell. The livelihoods of these schools depended on the fees paid by students that the schools were able to attract. Because these schools were unsupervised by the community, the regulations found in them were often invented or derived from custom. The curriculum often revolved around the sciences and the practical skills of engineering, navigation, and surveying. Entrepreneurial schools contributed socially by laying a foundation for the practical engineering profession, thereby creating a new class of skilled people (Good & Teller, 1973).

The church charity school system provided the nearest semblance of a free school system in the American colonies prior to the Revolutionary War. These schools were typically open to the poorer residents, who were members of the Anglican church. According to E. P. Cubberley (1962), the church charity school idea "largely dominated such education as was provided, with the apprenticing of orphans always a prominent feature, and a 'free school' supported by assessments, found here and there with a master 'capable of teaching the learned languages and the useful parts of Mathematics'" (p. 24).

Immigration patterns, dispersion of population, and unstable family life due to high mortality rates in the South resulted in fewer schools and less effective family instruction than in the New England or the middle colonies. Schooling in the South was dominated by the Society for the Preservation of the Gospel in Foreign Parts (SPG), which was established in 1701, and by old field schools (Carper, 1995). The SPG was developed in London with the hope that it could help channel large numbers of missionaries into the colonies. In particular, the SPG was dedicated to the propagation of the gospel in America. The SPG established 169 mission-ary stations that extended from New Hampshire to Georgia. More than 80 schoolmasters and 18 catechists taught charity school children to "'read, write, and cast accounts,' leading prayers in the absence of the clergy, and itinerating in the cause of Anglicanism" (Cremin, 1970, p. 342). The SPG also distributed bibles, prayer books, sermons, devotional works, and school texts in a variety of languages. Teachers of the SPG were intended to instruct children to live as Christians, teach them to read so that they might understand the Holy Scripture, and "teach them to write a plain and legible hand, in order to the fitting them for useful employments, with as much arithmetic as shall be necessary to the same purpose, to lead them in morning and evening prayer, to oblige them to attend church services, to exercise special care concerning their manners, to encourage them to be industrious, and at all times to set them appropriate examples of virtue and piety" (Cremin, p. 343).

Old field schools existed in the South until about 1850. The term came from the practice of placing schoolhouses in fields that had been overcultivated and were laying dormant while the ground recuperated. Often the only furnishings found in these schools were crude benches lining the walls and a high desk for the teacher. Old field schools did not differ drastically from rural elementary schools in other parts of the country (Cubberley, 1962). Teachers in field schools in Virginia were described by Cubberley: "Some of the teachers of these old field schools were invalids, some were slaves to drunkenness, most of them were entirely ignorant of the art of teaching and a terror to their pupils. There were a few who possessed culture, intelligence, morality, and ability" (p. 425).

Other Significant Developments in Colonial Education

The academy movement in the colonies represented a desire by the colonists to provide a more utilitarian education than that provided in classical grammar schools. In general, the academies had two primary purposes: to provide a useful education, and to provide social mobility for the average person. By 1855, Henry Barnard noted that there existed 6,185 academies in the United States. These institutions varied in curriculum and organization and were generally controlled by a mixture of public and private funding. Benjamin Franklin proposed the first academy with his *Proposals Relating to the Education of Youth in Pennsylvania* in 1749. The academy that was established from this proposal eventually became the University of Pennsylvania (Spring, 1994).

A very significant educational development occurred at the close of the colonial period. In 1779, Thomas Jefferson made his famous proposal to the Virginia legislature titled *A Bill for the More General Diffusion of Knowledge*. Jefferson held a strong belief that education could provide the tools and knowledge necessary to improve morality and reason. His proposal established schools that were tuition free for three years of education for all children, male and female, who were taught reading, writing, arithmetic, and history of the Greeks, Romans, English, and Americans (Spring, 1994).

SCHOOL DISTURBANCE CHARACTERISTICS

Early Colonial Schools

Behavioral expectations (Hyman & Lally, 1980) were very extensive and well defined in early colonial schools, most often associated with religious philosophies focusing on morality and development of character. Students experienced dull curriculums that generally consisted of recitation, repetition, and drill.

A very low degree of efficiency characterized early colonial schools. School hours were long and were void of any liberal attitude in instruction because of the intensive religious motive that education was attempting to serve. In addition, most school time was wasted because of an almost complete lack of teaching equipment, supplies, or even books. Schoolmasters were required to use extremely poor methods of teaching. The typical schoolhouse was built of logs with rough puncheon floors. Usually, seats and a rough board desk lined the walls. Often paper, greased with lard, was placed inside window frames instead of glass. There were never any blackboards or maps, and slates were not used until about 1820 (Cubberley, 1934).

Uniformly prohibited behavior (Hyman & Lally, 1980) in students consisted of borrowing or lending, climbing, balancing a pen on the ear, spitting on the floor, or leaving a seat without permission. The consequences of student nonconformity were clearly spelled out in colonial schoolhouses, usually taking the form of lashes for offenses such as boys and girls playing together, failing to bow to strangers, or name-calling.

Dominant Beliefs

The dominant belief in the colonies that a child's nature was inherently evil justified the authoritarian education of this time. Because it was believed that a child was prone to sin, the best way to keep him under control was to instill a fear of the drastic consequences of breaking God's laws or committing sin. This belief, in turn, moved the concepts of fear, discipline, and unconditional obedience into the classrooms (Butts & Cremin, 1953).

Few individuals or families in colonial times commanded the resources, tools, or labor that would free them from dependence on their neighbors. In this veritable hand-to-mouth existence, cooperation was vital. Most people were Protestant and worshipped at the same church. In many parts of the country, particularly New England, there were few outsiders to intrude on the daily routine of the average citizen. Frequent marriages turned many neighbors into relatives, and daily contact with a limited number of people fostered reliance on strong, informal social control. In short, the environmental conditions of the time produced a kind of community interdependence and insularity that facilitated local community control, an emphasis on individual responsibility, and a distrust of outside influence (Rothman, 1971).

Life was dominated by a network of three major social institutions: family, church, and community. The family was to raise children to respect the law and authority, the church was to oversee not only family discipline but also adult behavior, and members of the community were to supervise each other to detect and correct the first signs of deviancy (Rothman, 1971).

The colonists were concerned about deviant behavior and adopted harsh methods for dealing with it; however, they did not see deviant behavior as a critical social problem in the sense that they blamed themselves or their communities for it, nor did they expect to eliminate it. Crime and evil, they believed, were inherent in people and, therefore, endemic to society (Rothman, 1971).

John Cotton, one of the most influencial spokesmen of the early Puritan movement, wrote short catechisims designed to teach children that their inherent corruption bent them toward sin, where death and damnation were to be found. Cotton interpreted the commandment to "Honor thy father and thy mother" to mean that children must offer total obedience to all of their superiors in family, church, state, and, especially in school. He believed in education as a means of inculcating proper behavior and obedience in children; the law would take care of those children who would not bend their wills to the rules. In 1641 Cotton drew up, as part of his proposal of a new code of laws to be considered by the Massachusetts General Court, a passage to deal with habitually unruly children: "Rebellious children, whether they continue in riott or drunkenesse, after due correction from their parents, or whether they curse or smite their parents, to be put to death" (Butts & Cremin, 1953, p. 67).

In 1699, Cotton Mather published a book titled *A Family Well-Ordered*, which was divided into two parts: one addressed to parents, the other to children. In the first section, parents were warned to care for the salvation of their children. This section argued that the only way to achieve this goal was for parents to keep their children in subjection, and parental word was law (Butts & Cremin, 1953).

The second part of the book detailed the duties of the child to the parents. Being cursed by God was the primary threat against children, and if they sinned, they would experience untimely death or suicide and would be eaten by vultures. This punishment would continue into the afterlife, as the child would be placed into the eternal darkness of hell. Mather carried these beliefs into the school as he suggested that fear, obedience, discipline, and absolute authority were the essential parts of colonial instruction (Butts & Cremin, 1953).

The *Massachusetts Bay Colony School Law of May 1642* is one of the earliest laws on education in the American colonies. It reflected the concern of the New England settlers, even at that early date, with establishing a uniform code of education and confirmed an awareness that family responsibility for education had been, for the most part, a failure. The southern colonies, on the other hand, were less concerned with a public system of education. Geographic, social, and economic conditions resulted in a system of apprenticeship and vocational training for the poor, while the children of wealthy families were educated by private tutors. Both the *Massachusetts Act* and the *Virginia Act of 1646* shared a common apprehension that lack of education might allow children to fall into corrupt ways (*The charters and general laws*, pp. 73–76).

By the seventeenth century (Baker & Rubel, 1980), the religious doctrines of Protestantism and Catholicism had changed the prevailing attitudes toward children. The child was seen as having two conflicting images: one as innocent and one as the product of sin. Because children were the products of sex, which in itself was sinful, they must be watched and supervised constantly.

The seventeenth century also saw the implementation of a system of informing: Children were expected to report any negative behavior they witnessed in other children, both inside and outside of school. Any informer who failed to report an offense was punished as if he or she had actually committed the act (Baker & Rubel, 1980).

It was a primary duty of teachers to keep strict rules and good order in the classroom above all else. The ability to maintain order continued to be the most important part of a teacher's qualifications, primarily because the teacher often had to physically fight the larger males for control of the classroom. It was often a game to see whether the students could run the teacher off. Classrooms, not surprisingly, were often the battlegrounds for control between teacher and students (Cubberley, 1934).

During this period, a few people believed that children should be treated more gently and tenderly because they felt that those acts were characteristic of childhood. Others felt that children had rights of their own and should at least be treated as immature beings whose interests and capacities should be considered in the educational process (Butts & Cremin, 1953).

Many democratizing forces were set in motion in the United States in the eighteenth century. As the nation increased in population, it also grew in diversification among its people and, consequently, among the children who entered its schools. The growing school population came to represent a wide range of abilities, backgrounds, and aspirations, all of which had to be accommodated by public educational institutions (Goodlad, 1967).

Discipline

Treatment was severe in all classes, and a large portion of the school day was spent on imposing discipline. In lower level schools, children were subjected to little else than hard punishments. Most sketches of colonial schools show the schoolmaster holding a bundle of switches. This depiction sent the message that a schoolmaster had to be able and willing to impose order in the classroom. There was never any consideration that there might be a correlation among severe punishment, poorly taught students, and unruly classrooms (Cubberley, 1934).

The colonial era in America saw disobedient children being tied to whipping posts and beaten. Whipping posts were very often set up in the classroom or in the yard or street outside. Whipping was seen as a teaching tool, and such violence against children was justified in part by Scripture. For instance, Proverbs 6 and 15 in the King James version of the Old Testament state, "He that spareth his rod hateth his son; but he that loveth him chastiseth him betimes" and "Foolishness is bound up in the heart of a child; but the rod of correction shall drive it far from him" (Regoli & Hewitt, 1994, p. 252).

The most common punishments for children were fines and the whip, but wide use was made of mechanisms of shame such as the stocks, the pillory, and, occasionally, branding. Both the stocks and the pillory were located in a public place. In both, the child would be subjected to physical pain and discomfort and to public scorn and ridicule. Branding offenders with a "T" for thief, a "B" for blasphemy, or an "A" for adultery was also used. The criminal codes prescribed a long list of death-penalty offenses: arson, horse-stealing, robbery, burglary, sodomy, and murder, among many others (Barnes, 1972). Caning was a commonly accepted practice and widely used.

If a family was unable to control or educate its own children to the satisfaction of town officials, the officials had the power to remove those children from their homes and to place them in homes where they would receive a decent and Christian education (Rothman, 1971).

Although Puritan child-raising practices were by no means universal throughout the colonies, the moralistic principles they espoused seem to have had a great impact on subsequent generations of nineteenth-century reformers: the principles stressing obedience, submission to authority, hard work, modesty, and chastity. Furthermore, the small towns in which the colonists lived were admirably suited to an implementation of these principles (Rothman, 1971).

There was no distinct legal category termed "juvenile delinquency" in the eighteenth century. Americans still relied on English common law, which specified that children under the age of seven could not be guilty of a serious crime. Between the ages of eight and fourteen, children might be presumed innocent unless proven otherwise. Juries were expected to pay close attention to the child, and, if he was capable of discerning the nature of his sins, he could be convicted and even sentenced to death. In most of the colonies, anyone over the age of 14 was judged as an adult (Rothman, 1971).

There were established forbidden criminal offenses dealing only with juveniles: rebelliousness, disobedience, sledding on the Sabbath, or playing ball on public streets. In some colonies, the penalty for rebelliousness against parents was death. In actual practice, however, the courts and juries were often lenient toward the young. Children were often acquitted after a nominal trial or pardoned if found guilty. Some young children were severely punished or even put to death, but it was a rare occurrence (Rothman, 1971).

Colonial social organization did not survive for long in the nineteenth century. After the Revolutionary War, Americans were subjected to a series of changes that were overwhelming to many while altering irrevocably the tightly knit communities to which they were accustomed.

Any punishments against students were ultimately justified by the Puritan belief that the education of their children was a vital responsibility. Students had to be able to read the laws of God so they could be saved from evil and gain salvation. All forms of corporal punishment were justified for the purposes of control and character regeneration. Probably because of the treatment of students, there is no evidence that any significant misbehavior occurred during this time.

The early eighteenth century saw a more reasonable attitude toward children and childhood continue to grow. The SPG instructed schoolmasters in 1706 to use "kind and gentle methods" in the instruction of their students so that they may be loved as well as feared by their students. It was also stated that when punishment was necessary, the child should understand that it was given out of kindness and reason, not out of a teacher's vindictiveness to maintain authority (Butts & Cremin, 1953).

The stubborn child still was dealt with severely, but only after other methods of group censure had failed. It was still felt that an unruly child should be beaten soundly and often as a standard operating procedure. It was also believed that shy and slow-learning children could actually be harmed by harsh words and much whipping. This belief brought about one of the first movements dictating that teachers should humble themselves to attain community with their children (Butts & Cremin, 1953).

SUMMARY

Education of children in early colonial America was unsystematic, unregulated, and discontinous. The structure that did exist consisted of family, church, and school. Each of these forces was held responsible for the proper Christian education of the children in the colonies. Most behavioral expectations for these children were founded in philosophies focusing on morality and development of character. Instruction consisted of long hours in homemade structures that were dangerously cold in the winter and severely hot in the summer, in which students experienced dull curriculums generally consisting of recitation, memorization, and drill.

The early colonial period was known for its extremely harsh treatment of youth in and out of the school setting. The most common disciplinary technique was corporal punishment. Whipping was seen as a teaching aid. Children were also placed in stocks, stripped naked and beaten, branded, and even put to death for crimes such as rebelliousness and thievery. Commonly forbidden offenses dealing only with juveniles were rebelliousness, disobedience, sledding on the Sabbath, or playing ball on a public street. Most harsh treatment of juveniles was justified by Scripture.

3

Early National Period, 1780–1830

The period between 1780 and 1830 saw many conflicting views of how the new Republic should educate its citizens; the purpose of education itself came into question. Chapter 3 seeks to examine these issues. School disturbance is examined during this 50-year period in the context of how the first schools having large numbers of students of varying ages found classroom control crucial and, often, impossible.

SOCIAL DEVELOPMENTS

Socially, the early national period was a time of growth for the Republic. The United States saw developments such as the War of 1812, the Northwest Ordinance, and westward migration. The War of 1812, although fraught with significant losses by the United States on both the coastal and Canadian fronts, helped to renew national spirit. After Andrew Jackson's crushing defeat of the British at New Orleans in 1815 and the signing of the Treaty of Ghent, the United States experienced a surge of national self-confidence. One important American player during this time was Henry Clay. As Speaker of the House in 1812, Clay formulated an integrated economic program titled "The American System," which called for a national bank, taxes to promote domestic industry, and federally financed internal improvements. This plan embodied the nationalism that possessed the country during and immediately following the War of 1812.

Much of the plan saw a demise, however, when Andrew Jackson was elected president in 1828, and the new principles of laissez-faire economics were introduced.

The Northwest Ordinance, originally proposed by Thomas Jefferson in 1784, was officially adopted in 1787. It provided laws for the governance of the Old Northwest and admission of these territories to statehood. A significant part of the ordinance was that it provided public support for education. In addition to the Northwest, the Republic saw admission of New York (1795), Connecticut (1795), and Massachusetts (1789) to the Union.

Two of the most prominent actors of the early national period were Thomas Jefferson and Noah Webster. Jefferson did not believe that schooling should impose political or moral values; rather, he felt that once provided with the tools of reading and writing, the average citizen would use good reasoning in making political and moral decisions. Jefferson believed that the most important source of a political education was the reading of history and newspapers, not the schools. Jefferson also felt that a natural aristocracy would be formed through an educated leadership. To reach this aristocracy, however, the Republic needed to identify its future leaders at an early age and provide them with education through college (Spring, 1995). This ideology was most evident in Jefferson's *Bill for the More General Diffusion of Knowledge* in 1779, discussed in Chapter 2.

Noah Webster had a view different from Jefferson's. Webster was a strong proponent of nationalism whose legacy included political and social essays, a standardized American dictionary of the English language, an American version of the Bible, and his spelling book. Webster made his political contribution to the development of the U.S. common school between 1815 and 1819, when he served in the Massachusetts legislature and worked to establish a state school fund. Webster felt that his texts should, in addition to teaching reading and writing, produce patriotic U.S. citizens, develop an American language, and create a national spirit.

EDUCATIONAL DEVELOPMENTS

Unlike other revolutions, the American war did not result in dramatic changes in schooling. Education throughout the early national period did not differ drastically from that of the colonial period; however, because of fears of social fragmentation and an undisciplined citizenry, educational theorists caused a slow evolution of schooling throughout the early national period. Theorists such as Benjamin Rush and Thomas Jefferson proposed plans for state-supported free common schooling (Carper, 1995).

During the early national period, the line distinguishing public and private institutions faded even more. Primarily because of the efforts of parents, churches, voluntary associations, and entrepreneurs, public funding of privately controlled institutions became widespread. By 1830, except in the South, most white Americans had access to either private or quasi-public schooling. States, however, did encourage educational diversity. In addition to the district schools of the rural north, whose funding came from property taxes, tuition, fuel contributions, and state appropriations, state governments supported many privately owned institutions to promote civility, piety, and learning. At some time during the early national period, every state provided support in the form of land grants and financial aid to academies (Carper, 1995).

Public funding was also channeled to Protestant voluntary associations such as the New York Free School Society of 1805. These associations established charity schools in a number of cities. It was hoped that these schools would reach the increasing number of children of the poor who were unaffiliated with any church, as well as those who were culturally different and posed a perceived threat to the social and economic order. These societies laid the groundwork for what would become the urban public school systems (Carper, 1995).

Types of Schooling

The district system of schooling spread from the eastern states across the country as the frontier expanded westward. These systems were formed to meet the needs of sparsely populated regions where small numbers of children would congregate in a central place. The system was also used in cities where each ward or district had a one-teacher school and a board of trustees (Good & Teller, 1973). The district system represented a decentralization of school control as towns divided themselves up into smaller districts. Generally under this scheme, town authorities maintained control over the outlying schools but assigned a teacher to each district. The curriculum in these outlying rural schools often differed from that of the town schools because the rural farm family saw little use for subjects such as Latin. The rudimentary curriculum would therefore consist of the three Rs (Butts & Cremin, 1953).

Pedagogical confusion was characteristic of the district schools. Enrollments sometimes exceeded those in the city schools, but the schools only met for three to four months of the winter and three months in the summer. Students often supplied their own textbooks, which would consist of whatever a family owned. They would memorize passages and then recite these to the teacher. Because teachers changed frequently and there were no records, students often went through the same books more than once (Perkinson, 1995).

Charity and pauper schooling began to see a decline in the early national period. The pauper school idea had originated in the middle and southern states and still found some support there. The new West, however, exhibited very little tolerance of pauper schooling: Such schooling was derived from an English system based on class distinction and, therefore, out of place in the Republic, which followed the doctrine that "All men are created equal." Leaders of the new Republic felt that to educate some of the children in church or pay schools and to segregate the rest into pauper or charity schools was certain to create class distinctions that would later threaten the democratic ideology (Cubberley, 1962). The charity movement continued throughout the early national period, but it is evident that more children attended common pay schools taught by independent instructors who were not affiliated with any religious institution. These schools were probably not supported by public assistance and were attended by children from a wide range of economic backgrounds (Carper, 1995).

An example of the evolution of the pauper school to a less stigmatized practice was the Sunday school movement, one of the earliest philanthropic movements. Designed to provide minimum education for the children of the poor, the Sunday school movement originated in England in the middle of the seventeenth century. It did not show up in the United States, however, until 1786, when a Sunday school was established in Hanover County, Virginia. Shortly thereafter, a Sunday School for African Children was established in Charleston, South Carolina, in 1787. Sunday schools began appearing in every state, but the movement was particularly prominent in the South. These schools minimized class distinctions because they were open to all citizens, not just the poor. At first, Sunday schools consisted of a secular curriculum taught for most of the day. Churches soon opposed the practice, however, and succeeded in changing the instruction from a day of secular work to an hour or so of religious teaching (Cubberley, 1962).

Infant schools were established by factory owner Robert Owen in 1816 for the children of his employees (Douglass, 1940). Owen's schools taught "whatever might be useful and that they could understand. The instruction was combined with much singing and dancing to render them active, cheerful, and happy" (Cubberley, 1962, p.138). On good weather days, the children spent much of their time outdoors. No punishment was given, and no books were used. The system was soon formalized and regimented, however. Infant school societies set up schools for children aged two to six. These schools provided women teachers, who created a maternal atmosphere while teaching proper moral conduct (Perkinson, 1995). Infant schools were open year round and were intended to prepare the children for admission to grammar schools (Cubberley, 1962).

Academies in the early Republic provided education beyond the basics and included subjects such as Latin, Greek, mathematics, history, geography, and other sciences. Some academies had teacher training departments and prepared students to attend college. Students were enrolled from all social classes and genders. There were even a few academies that were established for women only: Troy Seminary, founded by Emma Willard in 1821; Mt. Holyoke Seminary, founded by Mary Lynn in 1836; and Hartford Seminary, founded by Catherine Beecher in 1828. In addition to the traditional subjects, the female academies sometimes offered ornamental subjects such as embroidery, dancing, music, and painting. All academies were usually controlled by private boards but publicly supported by funding and grants, making them quasi-private. The number of academies during the early national period virtually exploded. In 1800 there existed only 46, but by 1830 there were more than 1,000 academies in the United States. By 1850 there were 6,000 academies in the United States, teaching more than 260,000 students (Perkinson, 1995).

Educational Materials and Methods

By 1830, a revolutionary forum for educating the massive numbers of poor children in urban areas had been introduced. Joseph Lancaster, a British schoolmaster who had been unable to afford additional school teachers, developed a system of using student monitors. This monitorial system was so efficient and cost effective that it spread rapidly throughout England and into the United States. The New York Free School Society opened the first school using the Lancasterian monitor system in New York City in 1806. By 1825, the New York Free School Society had established 11 schools and educated 20,000 students using the monitorial method (Perkinson, 1995).

The typical monitorial school had between 200 and 1,000 students, who were constantly engaged in activity, in one large room. The students were sorted into rows according to ability, and each row was assigned a monitor. The monitors, in turn, reported to another group of monitors, and so forth. The monitors provided lessons from manuals and lesson plans written and developed by Lancaster, passing them down to the next group of monitors, who would then teach the next group, and so on. Most schools were divided into eight reading levels. The first level learned the alphabet; the second, words and syllables of two letters; the third and fourth, words and syllables of four letters; the fifth, reading lessons of one-syllable words; the sixth, two-syllable words; the seventh, The Testament; and the eighth, the Bible. Reading and arithmetic were taught using similar methods. In addition to teaching, monitors kept records, cared for equipment, conducted all examinations, and awarded promotions (Perkinson, 1995).

Monitorial schools were extremely efficient and inexpensive. Most students learned to read and write within a few months. There was criticism of this rigid, authoritarian approach to teaching, however. The military style of the Lancasterian method was unsuitable for very young children. As one solution, these children were sent to the previously discussed infant schools (Perkinson, 1995).

Teaching materials, as well as methods, evolved somewhat during the early national period. Textbooks that contained secular material rather than the gloomy religious material of the colonial period appeared. Thomas D. Dilworth's *A New Guide to the English Tongue* first appeared in America in the 1750s. It contained spelling words and fables and was, essentially, first in a line of spelling books. The culmination of spelling books was Noah Webster's blue-backed *Spelling Book*, published in 1783 (Cubberley, 1962). Webster's *Spelling Book* was similar to *The New England Primer* in that it also provided a moral catechism to teach the values that Webster considered necessary for maintaining republican order.

SCHOOL DISTURBANCE CHARACTERISTICS

Eighteenth-century Schools

In late eighteenth-century schools, boys and girls sat separately on wooden benches. Students were taught to read from the Bible and learned the Lord's Prayer; each school day opened with a hymn and prayers. Memorization of and reciting from the Bible took up much of the school day. Children who could not remember a passage from the Bible after three attempts were called lazy, and their names were written on a slate until they had made good (Butts & Cremin, 1953).

The smallest children began in spelling classes, where they practiced in groups so that slower learners could benefit. Once they could spell and read, children were advanced to the Testament class, where they continued to read the Bible but also studied arithmetic. Students still often worked in groups because it was believed that group praise or punishment would be an incentive for learning (Butts & Cremin, 1953).

The typical classroom in the late eighteenth century was still attended by a variety of age groups, ranging from five years to the teens. Discipline became critical, and stern methods of punishment often were used. The typical day would find students receiving praise for a correct answer or a blow for an incorrect one. The classrooms often were loud places full of undisciplined youth or cries from those being physically punished. To add to these problems, most schoolrooms were dangerously cold in the winter and extremely hot in the summer. Insufficent numbers of seats and other discomforts often aggravated students into disruptive behaviors (Butts & Cremin, 1953).

Eighteenth-century Views

In the early eighteenth century, Americans exhibited extreme fright and pessimism over delinquent behavior among youth (Baker & Rubel, 1980). There was growing public concern about the impact of vice and corruption on juveniles. Whereas the religious doctrines of the moralistic reformers of the past two centuries had suggested that people were inherently depraved and preordained to a particular destiny, the new philosophy was individualistic and stressed universal and unlimited human progress. Americans began to feel that some of the eighteenth century methods of social control were obsolete. Penalties for acts such as petty larceny were reduced; corporal punishments such as burning an offender's hand, cutting off the ears, or nailing the hands to a pillory were done away with. No longer, said a number of influential reformers, could Americans abide the use of barbarous punishments, particularly for children (Rothman, 1971).

Early Nineteenth-century Views

In the United States of the early nineteenth century, discipline problems were daily occurrences in schools. Teachers often controlled students through threats, intimidation, and beatings. A sign of those times can be found in a schoolmaster's prepared list of punishments that he had administered during his 50 years of teaching:

911,527 blows with a cane;
124,010 blows with a rod;

20,989 blows with a ruler;
136,715 blows with the hand;
12,235 blows on the mouth;
7,905 boxed ears;
1,115,800 raps on the head;
22,763 nota benes with Bible, grammar, or other books;
777 kneeling on peas;
613 kneeling on a triangular block of wood (Regoli & Hewitt, 1994, p. 252).

The belief grew that deviancy could be traced to early childhood where, almost always, there had been a breakdown in family discipline. Orphaned children or the children of drunk or licentious parents were most likely to fall prey to temptation and vice. The typical road to crime was paved, first, by a lack of discipline, then by drinking, and finally by lawbreaking itself (Rothman, 1971).

Between 1790 and 1830, the population of the United States grew markedly, as did the size and density of several cities and states. Parents were warned by the government of the awful consequences of an absence of discipline and were admonished to take stern measures against any loss of family control. Nineteenth-century Americans were so sensitive to childhood and so concerned with moral matters that they stripped away years from adults and treated everyone as children (Rothman, 1971).

Adult prisons and houses of refuge and orphan asylums for children were built. Asylums for abandoned children had been used in England and elsewhere in Europe for some time, but an entirely new idea was that places of confinement could be used effectively to both punish and correct criminals and to substitute for the family and community as the best method for raising neglected children (Pope, 1995).

The first houses of refuge, designed to separate children in trouble from hardened criminals, were built by private philanthropists in New York City in 1825, in Philadelphia in 1828, and by the Boston City Council in 1825. The fact that refuges first appeared in larger cities was no accident; the older colonial practice of placing unruly or neglected children in the homes of neighbors was more difficult in an impersonal metropolis. Indeed, houses of refuge were to become family substitutes, not only for the less serious juvenile problem but also for children who were defined as problems: the runaways, the disobedient or defiant children, and the vagrants who were in danger of falling prey to loose women, taverns, gambling halls, or theaters (Rothman, 1971).

Orphan asylums appeared at about the same time. The practice of incarceration seemed so effective to officials that it was used as a wide net that was cast for any child who did not have a proper home. Besides abandoned and orphaned children, orphan asylums accepted the children of women without husbands or children whose parents were alive but poor. Such children, reformers reasoned, should not be penalized merely because they were the offspring of degenerates or paupers (Philadelphia House of Refuge, 1835).

According to the concept of "parens patriae," derived from English tradition, the state could intervene to protect the rights of children and to assume the parental role, should that prove necessary. The destitute child was but one short step from becoming the worst nightmare of all, a lawbreaker. Thus, the only way to save the child was to remove him from the surrounding vice and to place him under the control of one of society's superparents. The saviors of U.S. children felt not only justified in taking this action but also morally superior for doing so (Rothman, 1971).

Before the Civil War, several states had passed laws requiring children to attend school, those under age 12 to be prohibited from employment, and the work day of a child over age 12 to be limited to ten hours. Although such laws were supposed to provide some protection for the young, they proved largely unworkable. Employers ignored them; many children worked rather than attend school, and parents joined in circumventing the law (Pope, 1995).

SUMMARY

Increased national self-confidence was the main result of the early national period. Events such as the War of 1812, the Northwest Ordinance, and westward migration instilled a level of assurance that was needed to continue the growth of the new Republic. There was also much discussion about the role education was to play in this growth. Debate centered on the rich and poor and how to educate them equally, in keeping with the ideology of "All men are created equal."

School disturbances during this period occurred in reaction more to conditions of the early schoolhouses and to teaching methods than to anything else. There was little, if any, consideration given to how much the extremely harsh punishments handed out to students contributed to school problems. The aggravation of the physical conditions of early classrooms was enough to incite much of the misbehavior found in students.

4

Common School Era, 1830–1860

Probably the most important social development of the common school era was the rapid expansion of the U.S. economy in the 1830s. Cotton was "King" in manufacturing, and revolutionary methods of transportation provided the means of distribution. A sudden depression existed from 1837 to the early 1840s, but by the late 1840s the Northeast was a strong manufacturing region with steady production and output. The rate of urbanization peaked in the Northwest around this time, ten years later in the Middle Atlantic states. Foreign trade and immigration were at an all-time high. Thus U.S. educators stressed with renewed vigor the importance of teaching intelligent citizenship and industrious behavior in U.S. schools. Commerce during this time seemed to correlate with the written and mathematical literacy of society. The more widespread the printed word, the more schooling was encouraged, which increased the market for printed material, and so on (Kaestle, 1983).

The nineteenth century was marked by more immigrants, more urban growth, more mobility, and more social instability in the United States. Immigrant groups were seen as contributing disproportionately to the problems that continued to evolve (Joint Special Committee, 1863).

Native-born U.S. citizens were not only concerned about this situation but also were alarmed by the new customs that some immigrant groups brought into the country: different sexual habits, different marital patterns, and other ways of talking and behaving. Such customs were deviant by definition and contributed further to the belief that immigrants were an inferior lot and a threat to social order. The facts are that wherever people of different cultures came into contact, many distinctions almost inevitably were drawn (Pope, 1995). These changes and beliefs played well into the national fear of how to protect individual liberty while maintaining order. It was felt that without order, all might be lost. Education took on an increased role and was thought to be a way to reconcile the gap between freedom and order. A sound education was thought to prepare men to vote intelligently and prepare women to raise their children properly. Moral training was viewed as just as important as the traditional 3 Rs in the education of U.S. youth. Children were taught to understand the concepts of virtue, which usually meant discipline, sacrifice, simplicity, and intelligence. Ministers, parents, and teachers were called on to help establish a virtuous citizenry (Kaestle, 1983).

During these changing times, some teachers performed well and some did not. Memorization continued to be the student's major task during the school day, mainly to allow the teacher some control over increasingly large classes. Children studied at their desks and prepared to recite their lessons one at a time. There was a growing movement toward using older students to help instruct the younger children. This monitoring system became popular in the 1820s, but in rural schools the idea never caught on. Rural teachers were still in full charge of their classes and demanded absolute silence from their students. Teachers' pedagogical excellence was often judged by how quiet and orderly their classrooms were, not by how much learning actually took place (Kaestle, 1983).

SOCIAL DEVELOPMENTS

Two major events affected schooling in the antebellum period. The development of modern day political parties and universal white male suffrage sparked a need for universal white education. The rising sense of U.S. nationalism led to more international competition, which, in turn, affected education (Kaestle, 1983).

The antebellum period also saw a tremendous growth of Protestantism in the United States. The superiority of Protestantism became a central concept of the social ideology of the time, which can be summarized in ten points: The sacredness and fragility of the republican polity (including ideas about individualism, liberty, and virtue); the importance of individual character in fostering social morality; the central role of personal industry in defining rectitude and merit; the delineation of a highly respected but limited domestic role for women; the importance of character building of familial and social environment (within certain racial and ethnic limitations); the sanctity and social virtues of property; the equality and abundance of economic opportunity in the United States; the superiority of the American Protestant culture; the grandeur of America's destiny; and the necessity of a determined public effort to unify America's polyglot population, chiefly through education (Kaestle, 1983, p. 77). The Protestants supported a nonsectarian (and, therefore, non-Catholic) common school to solely receive public financial aid, resulting in a stigma of illegitimacy placed on Catholic and other private schools (Carper, 1995).

EDUCATIONAL DEVELOPMENTS

The common school era represented the first of three major eras of school reform and was characterized by intense political debate. The common school emerged as the major form of schooling throughout the United States — except in the South — and represented a dramatic shift from private to public schooling, with a stronger demarcation between the two. The era saw the assertion of state authority in public education, the establishment of urban school systems, and the use of the school as a tool of social control. It was believed that the common school could create a disciplined and unified population that could intelligently participate in the political and social life of the United States. Private schools during this time were viewed by reformers as entities that would sabotage the goals of common schools and were considered divisive and undemocratic (Carper, 1995).

The southern states were the lone dissenters in accepting the common school system, primarily because the lack of southern urbanization and immigration resulted in little change in existing ideologies. A slavery-based economy and social ideology still prevailed and, combining with a dispersed population and a planter-class belief that education was a private matter, resulted in the perception of the common school as a Yankee institution (Carper, 1995).

Horace Mann was the major educational reform leader of the common school era. In 1837 he became the first secretary of the Massachusetts state Board of Education, which essentially made him superintendent of all Massachusetts schools. In all of his speeches and his 12 annual reports, Mann sent the message that Massachusetts schools could only survive and improve through uniformity — in textbooks, curriculum, teaching methods, discipline, and management (Perkinson, 1995).

Mann believed that common political values must be instilled in all U.S. citizens and that schooling was the key to reforming society. He felt that all children should attend a common school that would teach common political philosophies, making a political consensus possible. A problem with Mann's approach, however, was that he assumed that there existed common political principles on which every citizen would agree. He also believed that public schooling would solve U.S. social problems by training children so that they would not commit criminal acts (Spring, 1989).

The common school movement was distinctly different from previous U.S. educational methods in three ways. First, it placed a major emphasis on schooling all children in a common schoolhouse. In theory, children from different religious, socioeconomic, and ethnic backgrounds could be educated together to reduce tensions among the social groups. Thus, the term "common school" came to mean a school that was attended in common by all children and that taught common political and social ideologies (Spring, 1994).

The second educational difference was the idea that schools could be used as tools for furthering government policy. This idea represented the notion that there was a direct link between government educational policies and the solution of social, economic, and political problems. The third feature of the common school movement was the establishment of state agencies to control the schools, which was necessary if political policies were to be carried out. These three features of common schooling showed the tendency of mid–nineteenth-century Americans to believe that human nature could be molded by training within a formally organized institution (Spring, 1994).

Horace Mann realized that the common school could help reduce friction among social classes. He understood that development of modern industrial society had caused a chasm between capital and labor that resulted in a magnification of class distinctions. Mann believed that the common school offered two solutions to this problem. First, although complete elimination of friction caused by class consciousness was not possible, Mann felt that expansion of consciousness across social bounds could help reduce the friction. Second, he believed that the common school would help increase general societal wealth, thereby reducing the conflict between capital and labor. This thinking represented the earliest consideration of education as a capital investment and teaching as the development of human capital. Mann felt that the common school, by increasing the wealth of society, would eliminate the problems of unequal distribution of property by improving the economic conditions of the poor (Spring, 1994).

Teaching materials continued to broaden throughout the nineteenth century, but some remnants of earlier educational periods could be seen. Horace Mann strongly supported the use of the Bible in schools. He believed that instruction in fundamental doctrines of Christianity could be accomplished without reference to distinctions among denominations. The laws of Massachusetts also required the teaching of basic moral doctrines, which were listed as love of country, piety, justice, benevolence, industry, chastity, sobriety, moderation, frugality, and temperance (Spring, 1994). Religious education was, therefore, based on a nonsectarian use of the Bible and broad religious principles (Spring, 1994). Other prominent texts of the time included the *McGuffey Eclectic Readers*, a series of six graded readers that were the first to be issued anywhere and were the most popular texts for more than 60 years. William H. McGuffey taught principles such as the worth of obedience through tales illustrating the misfortunes brought on by disobedience. The readers had a significant impact and probably were a major driving force in establishing the class organization of the graded school as it is known today (Perkinson, 1995).

The issue of segregation in the common schools began to command attention during the antebellum period. In many segregated schools, there were stark differences between the way white children and black children were taught. For example, black students in Philadelphia were still being taught using the Lancasterian monitorial method, which had been abandoned in the white schools. Interestingly enough, the debate over whether to integrate schools was most vehement between black separatists and black integrationists. While the integrationists wanted desegregation for truly common schools, separatists had two primary reasons for resisting: First, black children would probably be subjected to abuse and discrimination in the white schools; second, school officials would probably integrate the children but not the teachers, therefore eliminating black teachers from the labor force. This debate was illustrated in a Boston court. The case of *Roberts v. Boston* (1850) found its way to the Massachusetts Supreme Court on the issue of separate but equal. (This case occurred some 46 years before the landmark U.S. Supreme Court decision of *Plessy v. Ferguson* (1896), which upheld that segregation in U.S. public schools was constitutional.) Benjamin Roberts, a printer who was active in black educational issues, sued the Boston School Committee to recover damages for his daughter, who was forced to walk 2.5 miles past several white schools to a segregated black school. The state Supreme Court ruled in favor of segregation. In his opinion, Chief Justice Lemuel Shaw admitted that segregated schools did create a caste system but that the schools did not create, and could not eliminate, racial discrimination. In addition, desegregation was not arbitrary: It was based on sanctioned tradition and culture. Although defeated in court, Roberts and his followers eventually won in the state legislature, and in 1855 desegregation became mandatory. Society responded, however, with tacit public policies and residential segregation, which resulted in a de facto segregated school system (Kaestle, 1983).

SCHOOL DISTURBANCE CHARACTERISTICS

Nineteenth Century

Behavioral expectations (Hyman & Lally, 1980) continued to be extensive in schools during the nineteenth century. Male students were required to scrape their feet on a scraper, be punctual, and bow when leaving or entering a room. Female students received harsh treatment for their perceived misbehavior. For example, girls caught dropping their heads in class were forced to wear a necklace of sharp weed burrs for the rest of the school term.

Punishments were often horrible and extreme. Some teachers locked their students in windowless closets for whispering in class, and other students were tied to chairs for hours. The twisting of ears, snapping of heads, and slapping of hands reminded students that the most important school activity was sitting quietly in their seats. Some teachers of the time did not like the extreme physical punishment of flogging children but still defended punishments such as boxing ears, striking ears, or shaking heads. On the other hand, some teachers found the rod or whip preferable because there was less chance of injury to the student than when using one's hands (Kaestle, 1983).

During this time, new terms for state-controlled places of confinement were coined: "reformatories" for young criminals and "industrial schools" for destitute or neglected children. For law violators, reformatories added the indeterminate sentence, which allowed officials to keep a young person until they thought he should be released: a marking system for classifying offenders; and parole supervision after release (Drowns & Hess, 1990).

Educational books written in the middle 1800s defined the typical unruly pupil: almost always a very large male with an aura of lawlessness, who had shut his eyes to teacher authority, who was brazen faced and full of contempt for rules, and who banded with others for mischief (Kellogg, 1893).

Nineteenth-century Schools

A common description of schools in the late 1800s was as wild and unruly places, reportedly because of the physical conditions, teaching methods, and inadequate disciplinary practices. Teachers were poorly trained and poorly paid, but were expected to improve discipline in this chaotic environment. Corporal punishment was the method of control most often chosen by teachers, many of whom entered teaching because they could not find other employment. Some forms of corporal punishment consisted of locking students in windowless closets, tying them to chairs, and twisting their ears (Baker & Rubel, 1980).

In 1837, Horace Mann reported that almost 400 schools across Massachusetts were dissolved because of disciplinary problems. Mann also reported that in one school consisting of approximately 250 students, he witnessed 328 separate floggings in the span of a five-day week, for an average of 65 floggings per day (Baker & Rubel, 1980).

Some teachers in the nineteenth century were compassionate and gentle people who controlled their classes without resorting to physical punishment. Female teachers were less likely to strike their students than were male teachers, perhaps because of their female nature or because many students were larger and would not stand still for any type of physical punishment. Interestingly, many female teachers worked only in the summer months because most of the larger male students were working and did not attend school during this time of the year. As teaching began to be more of a female profession at this time, fewer children were beaten in the classroom (Kaestle, 1983).

Many U.S. teachers in the early nineteenth century did not remain long in the profession. Very little training was required, and the pay and working conditions were generally unsatisfactory. Teachers often had additional jobs working on farms or in taverns to make ends meet. Male teachers dominated most schools, and female teachers often taught only during the brief interludes between their own schooling and marriage. Still, some teachers were college educated or earning extra money by teaching while attending college. All teachers had bad reputations merely for being teachers: Most were believed to be drunken, foreign, and ignorant. Early school reformers supported this belief, pushing for more selection criteria and more thorough examinations for potential school teachers; they also pushed for better teacher pay, benefits, and working conditions (Kaestle, 1983).

Poverty spread across large U.S. cities in the years after the Revolutionary War. This economic instability worried the citizens, and the growing number of slums alarmed city leaders. Once again, education was seen as the solution to these problems. It was felt that the poor manners and deficient behavior of the economically disadvantaged were evidence of their ignorance and immoral conduct. The concept of charity schooling came into vogue at this time as an attempt to educate the children of the poor, saving them from that lifestyle and, in turn, helping the economic base of the country. Poor youth had to be taught to grow out of the mischief and wickedness of their parents. Without education, these children would continue to inherit their parents' vices (Kaestle, 1983).

Interestingly, many fought against educating the poor because it might take away from the worker base that a growing country needs. It was thought that educating the poor would encourage them to question their state in life and wish to break free of their economic status: They would probably want more, but they would still not be willing to work for it. Thus, it was felt that mass education would result in disorder and chaos. Others contended that as long as moral education dominated the school curriculum, the status quo of the country would be maintained. Furthermore, the poor would become better citizens but still remain orderly. The idea that children, especially the poor, could benefit more from kindness than from discipline, more from curiosity than from authority, and more from tangible objects than from words also began to spread. A new idea would soon find its origin: Education might prevent crime. People began stating that each time a school was opened, a prison could be closed (Kaestle, 1983).

During the late 1800s, a problem developed in education that would carry into the twentieth century: having to deal with parental complaints. School officials urged parents not to believe a child's version of what happened in the classroom because of a child's inherent bias and predisposition to lie. In classroom incidents that caused outside concern over harsh treatment, children were labeled as prejudiced witnesses with groundless complaints. Any student complaint was immediately seen as improbable. Parents who wanted to know what was actually occurring were encouraged to come to the school for the true story. Teacher authority was seen as crucial to the survival of children and of the nation; teachers, therefore, could not be questioned or challenged in any manner. During this period, it was reported that one of the major problems facing schools was the undue interference of parents with school governance (Kaestle, 1983).

The conflict between parents and schools would become a major problem for nineteenth-century schools. Many parents began to take their children's sides in cases of school discipline. Parents would disrupt school sessions to argue with teachers; in some cases, parents would physically assault teachers. Many teachers were arrested for beating a child under the guise of enforcing classroom discipline. Disgruntled parents often encouraged children to not attend school or to drop out. The first mass student protests against teachers (at the encouragement of their parents) came about during this time. Schools would see majorities of their students refusing to return to school until a certain teacher was removed from the classroom. Often, for the sake of the school, administrators were forced to give in and fire a teacher (Kaestle, 1983).

By the late 1800s (Baker & Rubel, 1980), teachers began to realize that there might be a direct correlation between teachers' violent behavior toward students and student insubordination. This was primarily the result of the large number of qualified teachers that began to enter the profession at this time. By the end of the nineteenth century, child savers were prepared to invest the problems of childhood with even greater rank and to give them an even more dramatic place in the whole of society. Perhaps the most striking evidence of this was the creation of the first juvenile court in Cook County, Illinois, in 1899 (Drowns & Hess, 1990).

SUMMARY

The common school era was a time of philosophical change and debate in the United States. Significant changes occurred in the economic base of the country, but changes in beliefs about the purpose of education and what was needed to ensure the future of the growing Republic were the dominant influences on education and children. This sense of nationalism would affect every aspect of U.S. society and draw attention to segments of the population that had not been previously examined: the poor, the uneducated, and the foreigner. Once again, leaders turned to education as a means of bringing these different people together to form the working class basis that was needed to help the United States grow.

How education should be used was a major area of contention during this time. Many felt that mass education of the poor would help build a strong economic base for the country, whereas others thought that it would erode the base. How the lower class could be helped while the upper class was not harmed was a major concern. Many wanted to help poor children but did not want to hurt their own positions in the process.

School disturbance during this time took an interesting turn. Expectations of proper student behavior continued to be extreme and the punishment very physical, causing many schools to become dangerously unruly places: places in which teachers were very brutal to younger children, while larger male students were brutal to teachers. Few female teachers worked in education during this time; of those who did, most worked in the summer months when many of the larger male students did not attend school. Male teachers continued to box ears, strike hands, and shake heads to maintain control of the burgeoning number of students. By the end of this period, parents would begin to look more closely at their schools and the impact of the schools on their children. Even though parents were encouraged not to believe the stories their children would bring home about harsh treatment by teachers, many sided with their children. Parents would interrupt classes to argue with teachers and, sometimes, assault teachers. Thus began a problem that would continue through the twentieth century: Should parents be involved with their schools and, if so, how?

5

Progressive School Era, 1860–1960

The next 100 years of U.S. history represented not only the second major education reform era but also a major era of reform in U.S. society. Commonly referred to as "progressivism," it is what J. Carper (1995) refers to as "a label for a wide variety of activities directed toward changing American social, political, and institutional behavior roughly between 1890 and 1920 in response to concern about a myriad of problems associated with immigration, economic competition, rapid urbanization, farm outmigration, monopolies, political corruption, economic instability, spectre of class conflict, privilege, social unrest, and plight of children" (p. 31).

The period between 1860 and 1960 would also see many drastic changes in juvenile behavior in society and, therefore, changes in school disturbances. During this time, control of classrooms would evolve from a tight structure around all student movement, to disciplinary classrooms and expulsion, to armed and uniformed police officers being placed in school buildings. School disturbance would increase drastically, causing these increased control mechanisms.

SOCIAL DEVELOPMENTS

The progressive school era saw massive reforms in all areas of public life, including the institution of pure food and drug laws, direct election of

Senators, women's suffrage, child labor laws, civil service reform, Prohibition, trust busting, city manager government, sanitation reform, and tenement regulations (Carper, 1995). Major events of the era such as the Civil War, the Major Depression, the Great Depression, World War I, and World War II affected views on education.

The Great Depression, in particular, had specific impact on schools and society. Some argued that society needed to reconstruct itself and create a new social order; this was to be done by schooling. The Depression affected the entire country; it was not bound by geographic lines. Traditional distinctions between urban and rural community problems were blurred in universal suffering. People began to think of city schools and rural schools as more similar, and the issue of the U.S. school and its role in society came to the forefront (Spring, 1994).

Americanization was the key to the progressive school era. It involved teaching the American language and customs to massive numbers of immigrants. In terms of schooling, by the 1890s the singing of patriotic songs, the reciting of the Pledge of Allegiance, participation in student government, and other patriotic exercises were implemented. Ironically, as Perkinson (1995) indicates, using the school as a means of creating political meritocracy or consensus — or even a sense of patriotism — could be construed as contradictory to the ideals of political liberty and considered distinctly un-American.

The impact of vast immigration and the industrialization of the cities was strongest on children. Traditional life patterns and sequences had been shattered; parents were unable to serve as traditional behavior models, and they felt that their children were growing up in a city wilderness. There was a strong belief that children had to be tamed and civilized. As Perkinson (1995) states, "These 'street arabs' should not be in the street threatening the life, limb, and property of law-abiding citizens. The school room was where these young hoodlums belonged. It was scandalous that many of these 'future citizens' could hardly speak English, let alone read or write it. They needed to be civilized and Americanized. Education was the only means to save American society from the threat posed by the urban masses" (p. 65). The children of immigrants posed another problem. Many of them entered the labor force and worked for very low wages, which caused either a depression of all workers' salaries or displacement of adults from their jobs. The emerging ideology was that there should be a law to keep children in school and out of the labor market (Perkinson, 1995).

EDUCATIONAL DEVELOPMENTS

It was felt that the stability of the economy depended on the careful training of children, particularly immigrant children. To preserve U.S. democracy, city children had to be institutionalized and compelled to attend school. Immigrant children were often unkempt and neglected, and they represented a threat to the worker and to traditional social customs. By 1900, 31 states had enacted compulsory education laws to deal with these issues. Compulsory education laws not only brought more children into the schools but also kept them there for longer periods of time than in the past (Perkinson, 1995). Therefore, more schools and school materials were needed. Public funding was secured for these projects; by 1900, almost 90 percent of elementary and secondary children were enrolled in public schools (Carper, 1995).

With the establishment of more schools, education as a profession emerged. The U.S. public had begun to take seriously the issue of providing mass education; as a result, experts were found to help run and maintain the complex schools (Perkinson, 1995). These experts were considered progressive reformers, and they fell into two broad categories. The pedagogical or social progressives saw the school as a community center: They believed in student-centered methods and used an experience-oriented curriculum. Under their leadership, the modern-day kindergarten was established, child labor and attendance laws were enacted, and school nutrition was implemented. The social progressives stressed community, democracy, and social justice. The structural or administrative progressives stressed efficiency, expertise, and economy. Under their leadership, society saw a centralization of urban school governance, educational decision making by experts, a differentiated curriculum, the use of school surveys, and consolidation of rural schools (Carper, 1995).

The new progressive leadership resulted in school reforms such as antimonopolies, social bonds, and social efficiency. There emerged a much broader curriculum, including an increase in vocational training. Comprehensive high schools and junior high schools were established, and these were marked by stratification and efficiency. Public schools emerged as integrative tools in the complex, modern United States, with issues such as credentialing, sorting, and broad socialization (Carper, 1995).

Probably the most significant progressive was John Dewey, a social progressive, who felt that the school could promote the growth of the individual and the growth of society. In 1896, Dewey established the Laboratory School at the University of Chicago. It was Dewey's belief that the school should abandon the method of teaching set lessons and should instead develop social cooperation and community life. The children in Dewey's school participated in real-life activities such as gardening, weaving, and creating objects of wood or metal, activities that were intended to develop their appreciation of the human need for socialization. The children joined in activities to solve shared problems and learned cooperation and self-discipline. The school was intended to work as a community and, therefore, the child would learn to function in a community. Dewey's school transformed the role of the teacher who, instead of being responsible for one small segment of a child's education, now had the responsibility of the whole child. Dewey's theory of socialization in the classroom helped not only to expand the role of the teacher but also to extend the role of the school itself (Perkinson, 1995).

The National Education Association (NEA) had its own impact on the progressive era. In the 1890s, the NEA was partial to the natural sciences as a secondary school program. The NEA established the Committee of Ten, whose purpose was to give parity to the natural sciences. The committee endorsed social Darwinism, a theory espoused by Herbert Spencer, a proponent of U.S. evolution. According to L. A. Cremin (1961), social Darwinism was the idea "that history is the progressive adaptation of constitution to conditions, or put another way, the adjustment of human character to the circumstances of living" (p. 93). In 1918, the NEA's Commission on the Reorganization of Secondary Education established its *Cardinal Principles of Secondary Education.* Unlike the Committee of Ten, this commission called for a wider variety of courses of study and the establishment of a comprehensive high school. The commission listed its principles as health, command of fundamental processes, worthy home membership, vocation, civic education, worthy use of leisure, and ethical behavior (Spring, 1994). Throughout the 1920s and 1930s, the NEA supported vocational training, improved rural schooling, extended health education, and extended student services (Cremin, 1961).

The issue of race in the progressive school era was significant. The South was still defiant of the common school system, and the Civil War dominated the region. In 1862, as a combative effort, 72 teachers were sent to Port Royal, Virginia, by the New England Freedmen's Aid Society. The American Missionary Society, an abolitionist organization founded in 1846, supplied teachers to follow the army for the duration of the Civil War. By 1866, this society was supplying approximately 350 teachers. These organizations are but two examples of the 79 philanthropic organizations that sent teachers to the South to improve education. The work of these societies was often in cooperation with the Freedmen's Bureau, which was originally established in 1865 as a federal agency, the Bureau of Refugees, Freedmen, and Abandoned Lands. The Freedmen's Bureau supplied relief for freedmen through provision of medical services and supplies, supervision of labor contracts, control of confiscated lands, and establishment of schools. The Bureau operated with funds obtained from the sale of confiscated Confederate property and set up schools, while other philanthropic organizations supplied teachers. Unfortunately, some of these teachers were newly freed slaves who were barely able to read and write (Perkinson, 1995).

After the Civil War, the South passed laws to control and suppress the freed slaves. In 1865 and 1866, all the Confederate states except Tennessee passed black codes, which were intended to limit freedmen's liberty in varying degrees of severity. Whites refused to send their children, along with black children, to amalgamated schools established by Northerners, which resulted in the first de facto segregated schools. The Yankee school teacher taught the black child that Northerners were their friends and that the Republican Party was their benefactor. Children were expected to support their benefactors later, at the ballot box. To this end, the Yankees often used political catechisms to accomplish political aims (Perkinson, 1995).

Some whites approved of the education of freedmen. Planters set up schools so that their black help could be educated without outside interference. In this way, Southern whites could supervise the education of blacks. A few Southern whites argued that blacks would be made safer if they were morally and academically educated "Southern style." In addition, some advocates claimed that blacks would be better workers if educated. Southerners now considered education the key to white supremacy. As a result, Southern states for the first time established statewide systems of public education, which indicated how great a threat freed blacks were considered (Perkinson, 1995).

Blacks first entered the political arena during Reconstruction, with much of their attention focused on education. Black leaders demanded that their children be educated with whites; they felt that segregation marked them as second-class citizens. The Civil Rights Act of 1875, however, doused the hopes of many blacks that their position of subordination would be relieved once they were educated with whites. In 1896, the Supreme Court handed down its landmark decision that legislation could not eradicate racial instincts, establishing the doctrine of separate but equal schooling. The case was *Plessy v. Ferguson*. With court sanctioning, blacks were considered approved objects of aggression. Racism was rampant. The federal courts had cleared the way; Northern liberals were disillusioned and now viewed racism as the South's problem; and the Populists were disillusioned with former black allies. A whole new character of black leader stepped in with Booker T. Washington, who confirmed his belief that blacks should build a solid foundation in education, industry, and property. In 1954, the Supreme Court reversed its *Plessy* decision in the case of *Brown v. Board of Education of Topeka*, stating that segregated schools were unconstitutional.

SCHOOL DISTURBANCE CHARACTERISTICS

Late Nineteenth Century

The first juvenile court was established in Cook County, Illinois, in 1899 with the passage of the Juvenile Court Act. This act established separate proceedings for adults and juveniles, operating under the concept of "parens patriae" (sometimes referred to as "in loco parentis," which means "in place of the parent"). Juvenile court had jurisdiction over dependent youth, neglected youth, and status offenders. The goal of this system was to remove the stigma associated with the adult system and encompass a social welfare and treatment perspective in determining what was best for the child. This interest did not include the concern for constitutional rights and due process found in the adult system; instead, it was meant to be an informed and expedient process (Pope, 1995).

In the late 1800s and early 1900s, most rural schools were still not segmented into grades and had small student numbers. Discipline and order were reported to be of much less concern in these schools than in graded schools of the more urban areas. Many rural schools were reported to have between 300 and 800 students. Teachers felt that order and discipline were necessary down to the last detail for their safety and that of the children. It was felt that there must be punctuality, silence, and conformity in all student movement. Students were taught to be regular and punctual, not just for the sake of the school, but for harmonious human relations (Butler, 1910).

Students were taught to hold back their animal impulses to talk out of turn to their friends, thereby interrupting learning. A student was to learn self-restraint and respect for others. It was felt that as cities increased in size and industry grew, proper behavior in U.S. youth was essential. Rural schools continued to use harsh corporal punishment to control their students. Cores of teachers in the urban schools could secure good behavior by using structure, but the single teacher in a rural district had to do whatever was necessary to maintain control (Butler, 1910).

In 1847 a new style of school building was introduced in Boston with the erection of the Quincy School. In this style, each teacher had his or her own classroom of approximately 50 students. A new era in school discipline began, with the belief that it was now possible to manage a school with little or no corporal punishment. It was felt that teaching students to live without fighting would, in turn, allow them to develop into peaceful citizens (Butler, 1910).

Early Twentieth Century

The early twentieth century saw a much higher prevalence of and length in schooling. High school enrollment reportedly multiplied eightfold and was no longer for the few who were able to go or interested in going. A platoon system of dealing with the larger numbers of students was developed in 1914 in Gary, Indiana (Baker & Rubel, 1980). The style was not very popular as it was adopted in several areas of the country; eventually, it resulted in a series of violent student demonstrations in the New York City schools. Students would gather in groups of 1,000–3,000 to picket and stone the school buildings. Other students who tried to cross the picket lines and enter the schools would be beaten and their school books burned. The result of much of these demonstrations was that adult violence was validated as the preferred method of dealing with unruly conduct by children in U.S. schools.

Results of a classic study conducted in 1927 examining children's behavior and teacher's attitudes revealed that teachers regarded the most serious student behaviors as transgressions against authority, dishonesty, immorality, violation of rules, lack of orderliness, and lack of application to school work (Regoli & Hewitt, 1994).

1920s

Society was changing quickly in the first decades of the twentieth century. The 1920s were often called the first youth rebellion. This rebellion was not viewed with alarm because it was a wonderful time of prosperity and growth. The generation of the 1920s, especially its youth, began to question adult authority through increased independence and behavior different from practices of the past (*This Fabulous Century, 1920–1930*, 1988). All of these changes carried over to the classroom.

A breed of youngsters developed who claimed to be hard-boiled, heavy-drinking, and daring. The greatest changes seem to occur in females. Skirts were shorter than ever before. Cloche hats, silk stockings, fake jewelry, and bobbed hair replaced the osprey plumes, hobble skirts, and flowing tresses of the previous decades. The advent of Prohibition made clandestine drinking very appealing. Women also took up smoking, causing sales of cigarettes to double in the 1920s (*This Fabulous Century, 1920–1930*, 1988).

The morals of the U.S. public also began to undergo a revolution. More young adult males owned cars, with the result that traditional courting transformed into dating. Dating helped spark more daring fashions, scandalous dances, sensual jazz, and partying at late-night clubs. The older U.S. public tried to censure the behavior of the young, but with little impact. Young people were not concerned and continued with their plans to have fun (*This Fabulous Century, 1920–1930*, 1988).

The stock market crash of 1929 marked the end of the Roaring Twenties, the period of prosperity that followed World War I, and ushered in a period of economic depression, business failures, and unemployment. These conditions centered attention on all U.S. institutions and gave rise to a new way of looking at the relationships between government and economics that had vast importance for the future of the United States (Shepherd & Ragan, 1993). The decade of the 1920s had a lingering impact on the younger generation that would continue to surface time and time again.

U. Bronfenbrenner, analyzing research over more than a 25-year period (1928–1957), found certain trends in child-rearing practices among middle-class and lower-class parents. Parent-child relationships in the middle class were consistently reported as more accepting and egalitarian, whereas those in the working class were oriented more toward maintaining order and obedience. Although more tolerant of expressed impulses and desires, middle-class parents had higher expectations of children; discipline was usually handled by reasoning, isolation, or appeals to guilt. Lower-class parents were consistently more likely to emphasize neatness, cleanliness, and obedience and to employ physical punishments as disciplinary measures (Bronfenbrenner, 1958).

Bronfenbrenner (1958) concluded that middle-class parents were becoming more leisurely in accomplishing the tasks of child-rearing, while lower-class parents tended to demand middle-class qualities of their children, such as compliance and control, that they did not possess. Bronfenbrenner contended that the lower-class parents were pursuing values usually regarded as middle class but that they had not yet internalized the modes of response that made these values readily achievable for themselves or their children.

1930s

One solution to school disturbance brought about during the late 1920s and 1930s was the use of disciplinary classrooms. A special classroom was established in many school buildings where students of both sexes who did not behave in the normal classroom would be placed for indefinite periods of time. Although mostly done to relieve the problems of the regular classrooms, some consideration was given to adjusting schoolwork and discipline to meet the needs of the misbehaving children (Cubberley, 1934).

There were also parental schools for students who would not alter their behavior after being placed in disciplinary classrooms. Incorrigible pupils from all of the schools of a particular county were sometimes sent to one central parental school. These schools served as the last chance for many students with behavior problems, before they would be taken out of public education and placed in state industrial schools. Parental schools had much more structured discipline and control over pupils (Cubberley, 1934).

It was determined by 1930 that specialized instruction still failed some students. State industrial schools began to grow in number by the early 1930s, with 1 in 350 school-age juveniles across the country being placed in these institutions. Males were separated from females, and in the southern states, black students were separated from white students. By 1930 there were 173 state institutions, with approximately 70,000 boys and 21,000 girls, 13 percent of whom were black. Many of these children were characterized as illiterate, feeble minded, and slow (Cubberley, 1934).

If state industrial schools did not control the disruptive behavior of juveniles, then the next step was the penitentiary for youthful first offenders. Such institutions were established in states across the country. Although one may not think these institutions were part of the educational system of the time, they were viewed as being so (Cubberley, 1934).

Before World War II, the major problems faced by public education dealt with the value of certain types of instruction in the curriculum (Counts, 1934). There was much discussion about the value of music, art, dancing, health, and recreational activities in school. Topics such as these dominated the discussions of the problems faced by schools and what should be done to improve public educational programs (Watts, 1938).

In the 1930s, vagrancy became the number one crime committed by children because of the harsh economic conditions created by the Great Depression. Many young people left their homes and lived in the streets. More than 250,000 juveniles, nearly all boys, walked through U.S. cities in search of shelter and food. The crime of vagrancy strained the resources of the new juvenile system that had been developed in Cook County, Illinois, at the turn of the century (Drowns & Hess, 1990).

The only true type of school disturbance that was documented in the late 1930s and early 1940s was truancy. As early as 1939, the relationship between truancy and juvenile delinquency was being investigated. A study conducted by the New Jersey Juvenile Delinquency Commission (1972) found that of 2,021 prison and correctional institution inmates in that state, two of every five had first been committed for truancy.

When teachers were asked in the 1930s to describe a problem child, they reported characteristics such as antagonistic to authority, not applying self to school work, and dishonesty. It was felt that boys had more behavior problems than girls. When asked to report the student misbehaviors that disrupted schools, teachers listed immorality, dishonesty, disobedience, disorderliness, and failure to learn (Douglass, 1940).

In the 1930s it was estimated that 200,000 children appeared in juvenile court each year. Boys were guilty of offenses such as stealing, running away, truancy, and excessive lying. For girls, the leading offense was immorality (Douglass, 1940).

There was also growing concern over what caused problems in student behaviors. It was suggested that students exhibiting behavioral problems in the classroom should be given a physical examination, an intelligence test, and a psychiatric examination. The student's entire school life should be investigated, home influences traced, and friends and their behavior identified. It was felt that somewhere in a combination of these factors, the causes of the misbehavior could be found (Douglass, 1940).

Weak family control was one area that received much attention from educators in the 1930s. Some educators believed that the family could appear normal but in fact be very slack in child discipline or knowledge of the child's behavior. The social problems of separation, divorce, and untimely deaths began to draw attention in examinations of the causes of student misbehavior. There was growing evidence of the impact that unstable home lives could have on children and their learning (Counts, 1934).

It was also felt that it was natural for a boy to seek companionship and adventure with another male of the same age, but that this companionship could have negative impacts on both children. If the relationship were one that fostered delinquency or illegal behavior, then this behavior would be amplified by more and more boys coming together. Boys will most often attempt to shock and out-do each other by engaging in risky, dangerous, and often illegal behavior. The first time the term gang is used is at this time, in explanations of how companionship can move from the communities into the schools (Douglass, 1940).

1940s

Two great upheavals, international in scope, overshadowed everything that happened in the United States in the period between 1930 and 1945: the Great Depression and World War II. These two periods of national emergency caused new developments in science and technology, brought about changes in policies of the national government, and placed increased responsibilities on the public schools (Shepherd & Ragan, 1993).

World War II placed heavy demands on U.S. social and economic institutions and increased the responsibilities of the schools. Selective Service records reveal that a disturbing number of young men were physically or mentally unfit to serve in the armed forces; however, this did not prevent U.S. troops from fighting in almost every quarter of the globe, developing a two-ocean fleet and a global air force. The United States came into its own as a major power, and the country became the arsenal as well as the breadbasket of the Free World. Teachers left classrooms to take their places in the armed forces and in war industries, while food rationing and other war-related services were added to the duties of those who remained at home and in classrooms. The armed services, meanwhile, developed new instructional media and methods of teaching. At the close of the war, teaching had risen to a new position of importance and recognition in U.S. culture (Shepherd & Ragan, 1993).

On August 5 and 8, 1945, atomic bombs were dropped on Hiroshima and Nagasaki, bringing an end to World War II. People began to realize that a new era had been born in which many of the methods and products of the past would soon be obsolete. It would become necessary for humans to learn faster than ever before if society was to remain intact (Shepherd & Ragan, 1993).

A study conducted in the mid-1990s examined the leading school discipline problems in the 1940s. The following were the most frequently reported school disturbance incidents: talking, chewing gum, making noise, running in the hallways, getting out of place in line, wearing improper clothing, and not putting paper in wastebaskets (Goldstein, Apter, & Harootunian, 1994).

It was felt that many disruptive behaviors were not intellectual in nature; by teaching students simple virtues such as industry, truthfulness, and honesty, these behaviors could be overcome (Stendler, 1949).

According to a study by C. B. Stendler (1949), a majority of teachers felt that behavior problems in the classroom should be handled through constructive measures such as adjusting work, praising, encouraging, and studying the child to find underlying causes of behavior.

1950s

The 1950s saw a revisitation of the Jacksonian democratic ideal of education for the masses and the idea that education for all can provide equal opportunity for all. Prior to this decade, the purpose of school had been to instruct children in academic subjects, primarily for the purpose of enabling them to become literate and knowledgeable. During this time there came a renewed interest in a secondary purpose of education: to inculcate common standards and forms of behavior in the young for the purpose of preparing them to assume productive roles in a democratic society. Educators began to believe that the school and the home should supplement each other in these purposes because the child brings his home to school, and the school comes home with the child (Taba, 1962).

The common perception of the purpose of education in the 1950s was to maintain society and to perpetuate the "American way of life" (Addicott, 1958). It was felt that to do this, U.S. classrooms had to mold the type of disciplined behavior necessary for effective living in a democratic society. The common good was promoted by ideas such as democracy and required disciplined behavior and self-control for the general welfare of the country.

A dropout problem that suggested schools were not meeting these goals developed in the 1950s. In a study of schools, it was found that dropout rates, even in elementary schools, were 15.5 per 10,000 children for families earning $3,000–$5,000 annually, and 3 per 10,000 children for families earning $5,000–$7,000. For families making more than $9,000, the rate was less than 1 child in 10,000. In high schools, the overall rates were much higher (Sexton, 1961).

A typical sign of the times in the 1950s can be found in the writings and actions of Frederic Wertham. Comic books came under much fire and were attacked at the urging of Wertham in his book, *Seduction of the Innocent*. The book contended that U.S. children were being manipulated to perverse ends by the comic books. Wertham's book led to the U.S. Senate investigation of comics in 1954. Suddenly the comic book, once the province of childhood fun and fantasy, was being used as propaganda for a censorship battle that resembled the tactics of Senator Joseph McCarthy's hunt for communists in the United States (Decker & Groth, 1983).

Wertham did not use traditional scientific methodologies to support his charges. The fact that many mentally disturbed youngsters read comic books was enough to suggest to him that the comics themselves were causing juvenile delinquency. Certainly the comics featured some strong topics, at times. Drug addicts were often presented in the "hellish cold sweat of their frenzied withdrawals." Horror stories contained the typical bloody carnage, and the crime comics often made crime seem exciting (Decker & Groth, 1983, p. 62).

After World War II, the United States reversed its policy of isolationism and embarked on a new plan to become the leader of the Free World. The U.S. population increased rapidly during this time, resulting in significant shifts from rural to urban and suburban living. Overcrowded classrooms, shortages of well-qualified teachers, and half-day sessions became common (Shepherd & Ragan, 1993).

Because of wartime priorities, few civilian dwellings had been built during the preceding years. The government had promised 2.7 million new houses by 1948, but in the meantime President Truman begged the public to find living space for veterans (*This Fabulous Century, 1940–1950*, 1988). It began to appear that many returning soldiers were not prepared for homecoming, and much of the United States was not ready for the arrival of large numbers of discharged soldiers.

Returning to civilian employment was less of a problem than many had anticipated, however. Some veterans set up their own businesses with government loans and money they had saved in the service. Others returned to their old trades or went to college on the more than $500 yearly tuition plus living allowance ($90 a month for married men) provided by a new law called the G.I. Bill of Rights. As with any war, some veterans returned with physical and emotional scars, but most quickly adopted and began to enjoy the new gadgets they found in American life: television, entertainment, and fads (*This Fabulous Century, 1940–1950*, 1988).

Teenagers also entered a new world. Soda shops, refreshment stands, and drive-ins became sources of employment for some teenagers and hang-outs for many others. Two thousand drive-ins were built across the United States between 1947 and 1950. Teenagers finally entered a period in which they had free time to kill. Teenagers spent this extra time attending pep rallies, having sodas, smooching at drive-ins, going to dances at the gym, attending beach parties, skating at roller rinks, and engaging in countless other recreational and vocational activities. The most prevalent problem caused by these teenagers usually dealt with some type of initiation stunt for joining one of the many teen groups that were formed (*This Fabulous Century, 1950–1960*, 1988).

J. Hruska (1978) emphasized that technology and urbanization had significantly changed the twentieth-century United States and resulted in dramatic changes in the roles of youth. First, society had less need of their productive energies in the home because of processed food, natural gas, and labor-saving machines introduced by technology, computers, and adult workers. Because social relationships were heavily influenced by the production system, many young people found themselves severely circumscribed. As adolescents moved toward physical and intellectual maturity, they had strongly felt needs for meaningful work and social activities. During the 13- to 19-year-old period, however, they were (and still are) primarily confined to the role of student, essentially a staging area that prepared them for taking an active part in society at some future time. The role of student has been meaningful to some more than others. Perhaps a minority really enjoyed school, while many found school unbearably limiting and frustrating. Those who were unable to satisfy themselves with preparation for living in a democracy felt useless, alienated, and cut off from many of their peers and from the society that could find for them no alternative to attending school. Frequently, the response of these unserved youths was to wreak havoc on society and especially on those social institutions that most directly and personally rejected or frustrated them. School disturbance was one result. This condition continues to occur in the schools and classrooms of the United States.

The 1950s were considered one of the fastest changing of all decades for the United States. Many long-lasting and contrasting events occurred during this decade. Martin Luther King, Jr., helped organize a bus boycott in Montgomery, Alabama, and emerged a spokesman of the burgeoning civil rights movement. The young actor James Dean became a symbol for his alienated generation. Atomic scientist J. Robert Oppenheimer entered the decade a hero for his development of the atomic bomb and the potential it provided (*This Fabulous Century, 1940–1950*, 1988).

The residential neighborhood of the 1950s, as part of a child's environment, operated in two ways to influence behavior. First, the people in the neighborhood and the physical attributes of the area affected each child directly through actual contact. Neighbors talked to the children, sometimes actually controlling behavior, and communicated their values and attitudes; things and places that were available in the vicinity for use by children also affected them. Second, neighborhood contacts influenced other members of the family, who in turn taught children. In this society, families and children drew more cues for moral values, attitudes, and

behavior from the people around them. Thus, tendencies toward homo-
geneity in neighborhood groups increased — more so in suburban areas,
where contacts were frequent and of high intensity, and less so in highly
urbanized areas, where contacts were restricted and more impersonal.

There was also a boom in automation and education that promised an
upgrading of the labor force. This resulted in a lower proportion of blue-
collar workers, longer periods of training, and more employment in business and government bureaucracies. It was also expected that there would
be a more self-identified middle-class workforce that would actively
accept the prevailing ideology and participate in central institutions
through legitimate channels. There was also an ideological shift from
Cold War ideology that emphasized technological solutions to political
problems, to a consensus-oriented, mainstreamed approach in the social
sciences (Ash, 1972).

These developing times of the 1940s and 1950s broadened the scope of
educational objectives in the expanding schools of the time, including
pushes for students to learn a second language, use maps or polar projec-
tions, and begin studying problems of the world community (Shepherd &
Ragan, 1993).

Elementary school buildings constructed between 1945 and 1957
differed in important respects from those built earlier. Greater consideration was given to the type of program to be carried on inside the building.
There was a shift from two- and three-story buildings to one-story buildings; school sites became larger, and classrooms were larger. Much
progress was made in providing special education programs for excep-
tional children: the physically challenged, the mentally retarded, the
gifted, and social deviates (Shepherd & Ragan, 1993).

One of the most noteworthy developments during this period was the
rapid increase in the number of kindergartens. Enrollments in kindergartens in public schools increased from 595,000 in 1939–40 to 1,474,000
in 1953–54 (Shepherd & Ragan, 1993).

Although criticism of schools was nothing new, critics reached new
heights of disapproval during the period following the launch of the
Soviet satellite Sputnik in late 1957. Several factors contributed to the
criticism. The tremendous increase in public monies for education, made
necessary by increased enrollments following the postwar baby boom,
caused many citizens to protest their higher taxes. The flight of the middle
class to the suburbs brought about a concentration of parents who sought
status for their children through education and who demanded better
schools (Shepherd & Ragan, 1993).

During this time, the purpose of the school was to change children's behavior in socially desirable directions. The major concerns for educators were the concerns of children attending school: being physically healthy, wanting to acquire what the school offered, being capable of learning through school experiences, and modifying their behavior in the desired societal directions.

The issue of school desegregation became a prime focus of the nation's public policy debate in 1954, when the U.S. Supreme Court concluded that in the field of public education, the doctrine of separate but equal was unconstitutional. The Court ruled that separate educational facilities were inherently unequal and reversed the separate but equal doctrine that it had pronounced in 1896. Legal segregation, whether permitted or required, was deemed to violate the equal protection of the laws guaranteed by the Fourteenth Amendment. Chief Justice Earl Warren reasoned that to separate black youth from white youth of similar age and qualifications solely because of race generated a feeling of inferiority (Fife, 1992).

This movement was challenged many times in public schools and appellate courts. Token integration began as early as 1954 in some states, with strong hostility mounted in the Deep South and Virginia, led by the newly formed citizens' councils and similar groups. There was sporadic violence in resistance to desegregation and civil rights efforts in the 1950s. In 1957, Arkansas Governor Orval Faubus called out the National Guard to prevent nine black students from entering Little Rock's Central High School under federal court order. A conference between the President of the United States and the governor proved fruitless, and a federal court order forced the withdrawal of the National Guard (Fife, 1992).

When the students tried to enter the school, a hysterical mob outside forced their removal for their own safety. At that point, President Eisenhower ordered a thousand paratroopers to Little Rock to protect the students and placed the National Guard under federal jurisdiction. The soldiers stayed through the entire school year (Fife, 1992).

The following year, Governor Faubus peremptorily closed the high schools of Little Rock, and court proceedings continued into 1959 before the schools could be reopened. From this point, resistance only continued in the Deep South (Fife, 1992).

By the late 1950s, a widespread prosperity promoted the growth of an affluent U.S. society. Integration in the usual sense — that is, what appeared to be the likelihood that blacks would become participants in educational institutions — seemed doubtful. Blacks themselves welcomed this integration and hoped that the national government would encourage a pace of deliberate speed in fulfilling these developments in education, the economy, and the social order.

The nature of curricular reform for the elementary schools shifted in emphasis from better content, or more content, to the development of better functioning and self-actualizing individuals. Curriculum projects were designed to stress human nature, develop a positive self-concept, clarify values, reemphasize the affective domain, and emphasize early childhood education (Shepherd & Ragan, 1993).

The role of the school in the socialization process became even more crucial in view of the increasing inability of many parents to exercise as much control over their children as was possible in the preceding decades. As the effects of rapid social change and increasing urbanization eroded parental authority and influence, the school was forced to assume an even greater share of the burden of the socialization of children. Declining community interest in public schools as well as a somewhat conservative concept of the school's responsibility made it difficult for the school to take energetic initiatives in creating both motivation and opportunity for all children in career preparation (Shepherd & Ragan, 1993).

During this decade, the research of sociologists, educators, and psychologists revealed that the behavioral expectations that parents of varying socioeconomic backgrounds had for their children differed and were reflected in their child-rearing practices. These findings would set the tone of future problem areas for schools. The socialization process began in infancy in the home. By the time a child entered school, he had already internalized a particular set of values and a personal mode of conduct through identification with his parents (Stendler, 1950).

It was believed that the school had a supplementary function, but this supplementation must be realistic. The school's concept of what children need might match that of the majority of society, but a child's background might make it impossible for him to really engage in the school curriculum. The curriculum may conflict with the home's values so that to accept the school's offerings, the child must reject his home (Haan, 1961).

In general, many teachers demonstrated little real understanding of the basic principles of child growth and development; furthermore, they had not been taught the techniques necessary to develop classroom programs based on children's developmental needs, personal interests, and innate capacities (Oliver, 1953).

During the early 1950s, the following list made up the ten (in order) most reported school disturbances: stealing, temper outbursts, masturbation, nervousness, lack of respect for authority, cruelty, lying, fear, obscenity, and lack of responsibility (Stouffer, 1952, p. 271).

The NEA conducted a teacher opinion poll from 1955 to 1956, asking teachers whether they had been attacked by a pupil that year (Rubel, 1977). This poll found that 1,141 (or 1.6 percent) of U.S. teachers reported that they had been attacked by a student. This was an important study in that few groups during this period sought to estimate the amount of teacher victimization or school crime on a national basis. Between 1950 and the late 1960s, no nationally comparable records were kept on the amount of student crime.

L. Burgan and R. Rubel (1980) indicated that the first glimmerings of the violence that ultimately resulted in formation of internal security forces in the public schools began to attract public attention in the late 1950s. In ghettos of major urban centers, student misbehavior became sufficiently noticeable by the mid-1950s to warrant the U.S. Senate to conduct hearings in cities throughout the nation to determine the scope of the disruptive behavior. Books written in this era tended to lump misbehavior into the general category of "discipline violations," and it was not until ten years later that educators would begin to separate infractions of school rules from crimes. The popularized public view of urban school violence in this period was exemplified in a major motion picture, "The Blackboard Jungle."

Over time, students, teachers, and administrators all came in for increasing shares of harassment, intimidation, and assault. During this decade, buildings were defaced, vandalized, and even burned beyond repair with alarming frequency. Equipment and supplies were damaged, destroyed, and stolen at an immense cost to the taxpayers. As inflation spiraled upward in this period, taxpaying citizens' concern evolved into alarm over this senseless and nonproductive loss of property (Burgan & Rubel, 1980).

SUMMARY

During the progressive era of education, student discipline continued to be a major focus in the classroom. Teachers felt that order and discipline were essential to deal with the growing numbers of children entering their schools, and they began to fear for their own safety and that of their students. Children were taught to curb their impulses to talk to their friends and disrupt the learning process. During this time, urban school teachers began to find success in the use of structure in the classroom to control potentially negative student behavior. Rural schools continued, however, to use harsh corporal punishment to maintain the same control.

The first youth rebellion of the early twentieth century would see the beginning of youth independence and questioning of adult authority. One major change in juvenile behavior was the evolution of courting to dating, with the advent of the automobile. One reason Prohibition was enacted was to control the youth of the 1920s. Drinking and smoking were seen as major causes of juvenile delinquency — especially in female youth, who were beginning to exhibit behaviors that were thought to be male and unladylike.

The 1930s saw the growth of industrial schools and reformatories. Disciplinary classrooms were established to help those students who could not behave in traditional classrooms. Outside of the classroom, vagrancy and pauperism, much of which were caused by the Great Depression, were the major offenses committed by youth.

Truancy was the major form of school disturbance reported in the 1940s. A change occurred in teachers becoming as concerned with the students not in their classrooms as those that were. This period also saw a growing concern over the causes of juvenile delinquency and school disturbance. Inside the classroom, behaviors such as chewing gum, making noise, and running in the hallways were the primary annoyances for teachers.

The 1950s would see the idea of educating the masses to instill common standards and behaviors in children. There was a renewed interest in promoting the concept of an "American" way of life. School disturbances during this period consisted of stealing, temper outbursts, lying, and cruelty. A significant dropout problem in the schools influenced the major juvenile problem outside of the school: gangs. The progressive era set the stage for the myriad changes that were coming in the next several decades.

6

Kaleidoscopic Era, 1960–Present

The term "school violence" was coined during the kaleidoscopic era, as school disturbance evolved from a minor problem to one that caused many national education reports to brand the entire U.S. school system a failure. Disruptive acts committed by students would change from stealing and running in the halls to violent acts such as robbery and murder. These changes in juvenile behavior, combined with the public perception of a tidal wave of crime that began in the 1970s, would move the country to adopt a get-tough attitude in the handling of juvenile delinquency. The 1990s would witness the evolution of school violence into more violent and unusual occurrences.

SOCIAL DEVELOPMENTS

The period 1960–96 can be characterized as kaleidoscopic in nature, in terms of both social and educational developments. Major social events included the launching of the Soviet satellite Sputnik, the Civil Rights movement, the baby boom, the Vietnam War, and the introduction of technological advances such as television and computers.

Civil rights became the central U.S. issue just prior to and after the assassination of President John F. Kennedy. Lyndon B. Johnson signed into law the Civil Rights Act of 1964, which guaranteed certain rights such as voting and threatened to withdraw federal money from any program that discriminated on the basis of race, color, or national origin (Lazerson, 1987).

The baby boom made its own significant impact on U.S. society. Eighty million people were born between 1946 and 1964, drastically altering the demographic profile of the United States. These individuals were able to gain unprecedented cultural and economic power. Middle-class youth demanded entitlements such as material goods, special attention, freedom, and a college education. Students demonstrated in support of their civil rights and against the war in Vietnam, establishing the Student Nonviolent Coordinating Committee, Students for a Democratic Society in 1960, and the Free Speech movement at the University of California, Berkeley, in 1964. They shocked older members of the community with their outlandish dress and speech, drug use, sit-ins, psychedelic music, and violent confrontations with authority. Student demonstrations dramatically swayed public opinion against the escalation of the Vietnam War (Lazerson, 1987).

The advent of television strongly influenced U.S. society in the second half of the twentieth century: "Television raised the nation's consciousness about the unjust and unequal relationships in the society between the races, between the sexes, between the generations, between ethnic groups, and between the fit and the disabled" (Perkinson, 1995, p. 188).

EDUCATIONAL DEVELOPMENTS

In the 1950s and 1960s, U.S. education saw the establishment of high schools and college preparatory institutions on a massive scale (Lazerson, 1987). Schools were used as a panacea for a number of social problems: reducing juvenile delinquency through school attendance and summer schools; eliminating traffic accidents through driver education; improving family life through modern living and home economics courses; and eliminating drug use, venereal disease, and other social ills through health education. One reason that the school was touted as the solution to social problems was that it was the most available institution and the one least likely to affect other parts of the social system. The school was frequently the safest and least controversial avenue for social improvement (Spring, 1989).

The crisis of the cold war with the Soviet Union caught many U.S. citizens off guard and, as a result, the schools became a target of public fear and frustration. Suddenly it was very important for young people to be taught the skills that would be needed to support the U.S. economy and extend its defenses. The crisis reached its climax with the launch of the

Soviet satellite Sputnik in October 1957. As an immediate response and as a testament to the perceived relationship between education and national security, the United States established the National Defense Education Act of 1958. The crisis also resulted in the essential elimination of barriers to federal aid to education (for example, Southern fear of federal interference, opposition from religious groups, or refusal of state and local governments to relinquish control) (Lazerson, 1987).

In the late 1950s, the consolidation of rural schools allowed for more improved and efficient educational programs, better support of local bond issues for school construction, and intense recruitment of more talented teachers (Lazerson, 1987). Americans made the distinction that urban education was different from rural — and the rest of U.S. — education. Urban education and the problems associated with it received special attention. Most Americans accepted urbanization as a permanent part of society, becoming less concerned with socialization. Urban educators stressed projects and programs that emphasized vocational preparation. In addition, they expended effort on guidance and counseling programs (Perkinson, 1995).

The late 1950s and early 1960s also witnessed a curriculum reform movement that sought to bring recent discoveries about subject matter and new methods of teaching to the classroom. Particular efforts were made to change the way mathematics, science, and foreign languages were taught. Generated by cold war concerns over U.S. abilities in science and technology, the new curriculum movement was to benefit all students; however, attention was focused on the more talented ones. This began to change in the 1960s when awareness of the plight of the disadvantaged came to the forefront (Lazerson, 1987).

The landmark federal education development of the 1960s was the Elementary and Secondary Education Act of 1965 (ESEA), which essentially was a testament to poverty in the United States. The ESEA was based on two primary assumptions. First, living in poverty resulted in a cycle by teaching the children behaviors and attitudes that prevented them from gaining higher economic status. Second, children could be motivated and taught to develop the skills needed for higher academic achievement. The ESEA was particularly important because it clearly established educational opportunity and quality as a federal responsibility (Lazerson, 1987).

In a 1967 report, *Racial Isolation in the Public Schools*, the U.S. Commission on Civil Rights stated that segregation had increased throughout much of the country and that it was undermining efforts toward equal opportunity in education. The commission found that compensatory programs were not effective and that further desegregation efforts (for example, the creation of metropolitan school districts, magnet schools, and busing) were needed (Lazerson, 1987).

School districts were becoming more politicized. Federal courts no longer just espoused desegregation: They demanded integration and proof of efforts made to enhance educational opportunity. Between 1965 and 1975, the politicization of U.S. schools was unprecedented. Part of the reason for the intense struggle was that basic U.S. ideology was at stake. The ideals of equality, justice, and liberty contrasted with the stark reality of discrimination and lack of opportunity (Lazerson, 1987).

Scholastic Aptitude Test scores were given unprecedented attention between the mid-1960s and the early 1980s, embodying the concern that U.S. education programs were not effective. It was the hope that the use of these scores would enhance opportunities for talented young people who had suffered under inadequate teachers and schools (Lazerson, 1987).

In the early 1980s, two reports reflected the intensity of the equality and excellence issue. In 1983, the President's National Committee on Excellence in Education released its report, *A Nation at Risk*, which condemned the academic as well as moral decline of the schools. In 1985, the National Coalition of Advocates for Students presented its report, *Barriers to Excellence: Our Children at Risk*, and stated that educational opportunity should be fundamental to the ideals of U.S. schools. It stated that minority, foreign-speaking, and disabled students were still being treated as second-class citizens despite the efforts of the previous decades (Lazerson, 1987).

The decade of the 1990s has so far seen an increase in the number of federal programs for education-related activities. The following is a brief list of some of this legislation:

The Excellence in Mathematics, Science and Engineering Education Act of 1990;

The Student Right-To-Know and Campus Security Act (1990);

The Children's Television Act of 1990;

The Americans with Disabilities Act of 1990;

The McKinney Homeless Assistance Amendments Act of 1990;

The National Assessment of Chapter 1 Act (1990);

The Augustus F. Hawkins Human Services Reauthorization Act of 1990;

The School Dropout Prevention and Basic Skills Improvement Act (1990);

The Medical Residents Student Loan Amendments Act (1990);

The Asbestos School Hazard Abatement Reauthorization Act of 1990;

The Eisenhower Exchange Fellowship Program (1990);

The Tribally Controlled Community College Reauthorization (1990);

The Environmental Education Act (1990);

The Anti-Drug Education Act of 1990 and the Drug Abuse Resistance Education Act of 1990;

The Public Service Assistance Education Act (1990);

The 1990 Budget Reconciliation Act;

National Literacy Act of 1991;

Dire Emergency Supplemental Appropriations for Consequences of Operation Desert Shield/Desert Storm, Food Stamps, Unemployment Compensation Administration, Veterans Compensation and Pensions, and Other Urgent Needs Act of 1991;

Higher Education Technical Amendments of 1991;

Intelligence Authorization Act (1991);

National Defense Authorization Act for Fiscal Year 1992 and 1993 (1991);

High Performance Computing Act of 1991.

SCHOOL DISTURBANCE CHARACTERISTICS

1960s

In the 1960s, experts argued that antipoverty efforts, not educational reform, would reduce youth crime. The War on Poverty was conducted by the U.S. government to establish human resources and community-action programs. Many of these programs were directed at creating jobs for and training young people in poor neighborhoods. In 1967 the entire juvenile justice system came under attack. A presidential commission called the system a failure, stating that juvenile courts focused on petty offenses committed by juveniles while they allowed others to literally get away with murder. At the same time, many social critics charged that children were denied their right to fair treatment under the law because juvenile proceedings were held in secret (Drowns & Hess, 1990).

In 1964, a nationwide survey of public school teachers indicated that only 3 percent of the student population was considered a discipline problem; in 1967, results of a survey of urban secondary schools released by the Syracuse University Research Corporation concluded that disruption of education in public high schools was becoming extremely widespread and serious (U.S. House of Representatives, 1975).

In the summer of 1966, freelance multiple murder became the new characteristic U.S. crime. In two weeks, two shocking multiple murders occurred. In Chicago, Richard F. Speck murdered eight student nurses. Less than a month later, from the top of the tower of the University of Texas library in Austin, Charles Whitman shot 13 people dead and wounded 31 (Altman & Ziporyn, 1967). These occurrences helped crystallize public awarness of random violence and crime.

It can also be argued that, in the 1960s, the United States had become a country full of trigger-happy people. In the summer of 1968, a Harris poll found 81 percent of the people believing that law and order had broken down; significantly, all of the presidential candidates were promising to do something about it. The campaign speeches of Richard Nixon often centered on the statement that crime was rising nine times faster than the population in the 1960s (Graham & Gurr, 1969).

There were also people who believed the opposite. During the 1968 political campaigns, Attorney General Ramsey Clark received much criticism after stating that there was no wave of crime in this country, that statistics simply reflected the fact that the American public was beginning to dig into the reservoir of unreported crimes (Graham & Gurr, 1969).

Reporting in 1967 after an 18-month study, the President's Commission on Law Enforcement and Administration of Justice could not say whether the crime rate was higher or whether Americans had become more criminal than their counterparts in earlier times (Graham & Gurr, 1969).

By the mid-to-late 1960s, mass media began to pay considerable attention to numerous disciplinary infractions occurring in the schools, expressing concern that educators were not appropriately responding to this evident increase in unruly student behavior (Burgan & Rubel, 1980).

In the 1960s, there was no well-established classification system for grouping school-related offenses into categories that had any empirical scientific or practical meaning. Most definitions were restricted to either a small set of serious offenses or specific minor offenses. Better classification of data from individual and school records could have been used to discover correlations between rates of different crimes or to specify relationships between local conditions and criminal incidents. A very simplistic three-category classification system was eventually developed to compile the incidents that were included in reports of school crime. The three categories were school attacks, thefts, and suspensions; drug and alcohol abuse; and student protests and demonstrations (U.S. House of Representatives, 1975).

Wilkerson (Rothman, 1971) conducted research to determine patterns in the backgrounds of the juvenile delinquents encountered in the 1960s. First, most delinquents seemed to have histories of failing grades in school. Close to one-half of delinquents repeated two or more grades and thus became two or more years "over-aged" for the grades in which they were enrolled. Second, around 95 percent of delinquents had records of serious or persistent misconduct in school, with truancy as the most frequent offense. Third, a very large proportion (80 percent to 95 percent) of delinquents were school dropouts. Most of them withdrew from the junior high school grades as soon as they reached the leaving age of 16; few of them entered senior high school. Fourth, a substantial majority of delinquent youth expressed violent dislike of school, and at least another one-fourth expressed indifference toward school.

The following is a chart (Rubel, 1977) of the reported increase in some categories of crime that occurred in 1964 and 1968 at elementary and secondary schools across the United States:

Category of Crime	Number of Incidents in		Percent increase
	1964	1968	
Homicides	15	26	73
Forcible Rapes	51	81	61
Robberies	396	1,508	306
Aggravated Assaults	475	680	43
Burglaries, Larcenies	7,604	14,102	86
Weapons offenses	419	1,089	136
Narcotics	73	854	1,069
Drunkenness	370	1,035	179
Crimes by non-students	142	3,894	2,600
Vandalism incidents	186,184	250,549	35
Assaults on teachers	25	1,801	7,100
Assaults on students	1,601	4,267	167
Other	4,796	8,824	84

Source: Adapted from Rubel, 1977, p. 59.

The results shown in the table were compiled by the Senate Subcommittee to Investigate Juvenile Delinquency from November 1970 to 1975. The data supplied to the subcommittee by school districts were said by many to be incomplete, and little reliance has ever been placed on these findings — except by the media. These results made headlines in many newspapers and radio and television news programs across the country. These percentages have been placed in the literature as a hard fact, but many feel that they were grave exaggerations of what was occurring in the 1960s (Rubel, 1977).

Both houses of Congress conducted extensive hearings on the problem of school violence and vandalism in the late 1960s, and their reports on violence in schools shocked the nation. It was pointed out that there were 70,000 assaults on teachers annually, some ending in death. Among 757 major school districts, there were approximately 200 school-related student deaths in one year. According to figures presented at the House hearings by the National Association of School Security Directors, there were 12,000 armed robberies, 270,000 burglaries, 204,000 assaults, and 9,000 rapes in U.S. schools in 1974 (National Center for Education Statistics, 1974).

A conservative estimate of the annual cost of vandalism in public schools was $600 million. According to testimony before the House Subcommittee on Education in 1974, this cost included $243 million for burglary, $109 million for fire, and $204 million for other destructive acts. In 1973, the average cost per school district nationwide was estimated at $63,000 annually (National Center for Education Statistics, 1974).

The 1960s saw the first attempts at school safety plans. During this time, parents and paraprofessionals were used as hall monitors. Student leaders from all campus organizations were sought to provide peer leadership in school programs and activities and to represent the total student body when help was needed. Student grievances were heard when they erupted. Some of the first plans to control violence can be found in reports from this decade (Chesler, Franklin, & Guskin, 1969).

According to the *President's Task Force Report: Juvenile Delinquency and Youth Crime* (1967), juvenile delinquency was considered the single most pressing and threatening aspect of the crime problem in the United States. One in every nine young people would be referred to juvenile courts for an act of delinquency before his or her eighteenth birthday. Considering boys alone, the ratio increased to one in every six. Arrests of persons under age 18 for serious crimes increased 47 percent from 1960 to 1965; this number differs from an increase of 17 percent in that age-group population for the same period.

In the early 1960s, a few large cities instituted rudimentary security operations in their school systems. By the late 1960s, the successes of early experiments prompted a deluge of imitating systems. By the early 1970s, virtually all school systems serving cities with populations larger than 100,000 had implemented some form of school security in response to criminal and violent student behavior (Burgan & Rubel, 1980).

One effort that began in the 1960s to reduce the gap in communication between youth and police was the worldwide trend toward involving police in an ever-broadening preventive action in connection with juveniles. This trend was not one of deterrence and punishment, which had been the two principal functions of early police intervention programs. There began many different types of informal school programs in which the police participated, but it could be said that formal delinquency prevention programs were not in existence in many police jurisdictions. When such programs were instituted, they tended to evolve within a department as a gradual and informal adjustment to community requests. Formal programs appeared frequently as the result of surveys that had been conducted by forward-looking police departments. There was also a growing recognition of the necessity for training juvenile officers to understand children and their problems and to understand other disciplines concerned with the welfare of children (Kobetz, 1971).

The police-school liaison concept emerged during this time and was introduced into various U.S. schools. Two of the earliest programs originated in Michigan: one in the Flint Police Department and the other in the Michigan Department of State Police. Both departments were concerned with the alienation and hostility that existed between police and young people. It was felt that a police-school liaison program could improve communication between the two groups (Shepphard & James, 1967).

The method of classroom presentation was flexible, depending on the officers and the methods that were most suited to them. Games and simulations were sometimes used to get a point across to youngsters. The topics that the officers discussed in the classroom included the reasons for laws, the ways in which laws pertain to citizens, and the definition of law. There were discussions of criminal and civil law as well as a delineation of the consequences of a criminal record. Field trips to various court facilities in the community were made so that students could observe the different aspects of court administration and processing (Shepphard & James, 1967).

In the 1960s there was also a growing concern about the potential harm that schools were doing to children. Some felt that psychological damage could be inflicted on students who possessed low reading and math scores: the self-rejection that can result from the actions of teachers who avoid interpersonal relationships with such children and the social put-down effects of the negative terminology used by many educators to label such students (for example, "bad" or "dumb"). Many parents and educators considered these labels as damaging to a child as any fist fight, tire iron, or wooden paddle that might be encountered. There was also concern that this psychological violence was directed more toward poor and minority students than toward affluent students and members of the majority (Illich, 1971).

A group of educators harshly critical of U.S. schooling stated that schools in the 1960s tended to beguile the poor and the minorities with false hopes that their grandchildren would succeed, while implementing a curriculum that ensured the grandchildren's failure. Not only would the grandchildren lack a high-quality education, they also would blame themselves for not succeeding. Many critics contended that this phenomenon of getting victims to blame themselves for their failures was the real violence that was taking place in many of the schools in the 1960s. Critics also felt that teachers and administrators were failing to address this problem (Illich, 1971).

S. Cohen (1968) concluded that there was something wrong with the schools in the 1960s that had high rates of vandalism. He believed that the highest rates of school vandalism occurred in schools with obsolete facilities and equipment, low staff morale, high student dissatisfaction, and heavy financial burdens placed on the students (Cohen, 1968).

All of these attacks on schools and education turned into strong criticism of teachers and the roles they played in school disturbance and juvenile delinquency. Parents criticized teaching methods and materials. It seemed that everyone wanted to tell teachers how to teach. Broadcast media and the popular press constantly degraded teachers by stating that teachers in the 1960s simply did not know how to teach and that this lack of ability was causing many of the problems with juveniles. During this time, many teachers began to view themselves as victims: They received low pay, very little autonomy, and, now, lack of respect, while still having to perform the awesome task of educating U.S. youth (Perkinson, 1995).

In the 1960s and early 1970s, major U.S. Supreme Court decisions began to reshape the juvenile justice system into a more formal and legalistic operation that included many safeguards. The major emphasis of the Supreme Court of this time was to guarantee the same constitutional rights for juveniles as for adults. The court continued to recognize the parens patriae philosophy of the juvenile system but also believed that it was unfair for juveniles to face confinement without due process (Pope, 1995).

J. McDermott (1980) stated that it has only been since the early 1970s, with the growing emphasis on problems of disorder and crime in schools, that researchers began to examine fear of crime in school settings. Fear of crime in schools was a special concern because of the belief that everyone should have the right to safe schools, that safety is a minimum requirement in a positive learning environment. It was discovered that fear was likely to affect the concentration and academic performance of students, their participation in school activities, and their attitudes toward school, among other factors important to the learning environment. It was also discovered that disorder and uneasiness in schools were inseparable from wider social ills. There was a growing recognition that education could not be the great equalizer that it was once considered; that schools alone could not provide young people with life chances; and that inequality, racism, and sexism in schools reflect the social and economic inequality, racism, and sexism found in U.S. society.

During this period there were three good reasons for people to sometimes be concerned about a crime tidal wave. First, history shows that there has been a rhythm to criminal violence in the United States and that the rate of violent crime probably has been higher in the past than in the present. Second, crime scares are often generated by crime statistics that are very questionable and often distorted by the media. The statistics that are developed often do not justify the fear that society feels. Third, the Federal Bureau of Investigation's (FBI's) statistical image of a rising national crime rate in the 1960s had been translated into personal threats in the minds of many American during that time, creating a pervasive fear of strangers (Graham & Gurr, 1969).

In the 1960s, three significant reports related the causes, indicators, and resolutions of school violence to the family: the Kerner report, the Coleman report, and the Walker report.

The report by O. Kerner (1968) emphasized that U.S. public schools were not fulfilling the traditional purpose of helping pupils overcome their divergence in environment and background and that schools were not helping pupils utilize their different skills, motivations, concerns, and interests. Principals, teachers, students, and parents seemed to be highly alienated from the educational process. Finally, the student dropout rate indicated a terminal index of the degree of frustration and alienation felt by parents and students toward the school.

The report by J. Coleman (1966) determined that a child's achievement in school was affected more by resources in the home than by a school's educational resources. Minority and disadvantaged children started school with an educational deficiency, and the gap widened the longer these children were in school. Peer groups were found to have more influence than teachers. The report stated that a child's sense of control over the environment was the most critical factor in achievement.

The report by D. Walker (1968) discussed racism in schools in the 1960s. Racism was portrayed as existing in the curriculums, between teachers and students, between students and other students, and between administrators and students. Students were very aware that schools employed a minimal number of black teachers and counselors, that schools often failed to honor black cultural and political heroes, and that schools often avoided dealing with black families and black issues.

According to a Uniform Crime Report published by the FBI, there was an overall crime rate increase of 148 percent during the decade of the 1960s, while the population increased only 13 percent. In one year, 1972–73, there was a 17 percent increase in serious crime, including a 9 percent increase in assault and forcible rape and a 5 percent increase in murder. According to figures compiled by the FBI and local law enforcement agencies, offenders younger than age 25 were responsible for a majority of property crimes (Federal Bureau of Investigation, 1973).

The major trend in national crime has been toward youthful offenders. Figures from the FBI reveal that adult arrests for the violent crimes of murder, rape, robbery, and assault doubled between 1960 and 1973. At the same time, the number of people younger than age 18 who were arrested for murder tripled; for rape, more than doubled; for robbery, quadrupled; and for assaults, more than tripled. The percentage increase in youth crime outstripped the growth rate of the number of juveniles in the country (U.S. Commission on Civil Rights, 1973).

By the late 1960s and early 1970s, most of the violence in society no longer centered on radical student groups, ideological terrorist groups, or the war in Vietnam. Violence that evolved from clear, intentional, ideological bases was replaced by seemingly random violence (*This Fabulous Century, 1960–1970*, 1988).

Violent crime grew from 161 reported crimes per 100,000 persons in 1960 to 758 per 100,000 in 1991 — a 371 percent increase. The annual homicide total topped 20,000 in the mid-1970s; after a one-year drop, it grew to 23,040 in 1980 before declining for several years. The total began rising again in 1985, hitting 23,760 in 1992. The number of property crimes rose from 1,726 reported crimes per 100,000 persons in 1960 to 4,903 in 1992, with the worst increases occurring before 1980 (Office of Juvenile Justice and Delinquency Prevention, 1991b).

According to FBI statistics, children younger than age 15 were responsible for 201 murders in 1988 as well as 1,372 rapes, 11,345 aggravated assaults, and 6,470 robberies (Bureau of Justice Statistics, 1991).

In the early 1970s, Congress and the U.S. Supreme Court advanced the cause of gender equality. Under Title IX of the Educational Amendments Act of 1972, colleges were required to institute affirmative action. In that same year, Congress approved the Equal Rights Amendment, while the Supreme Court, in *Roe v. Wade*, struck down laws making abortions illegal (Fife, 1992; Shepherd & Ragan, 1993).

Divorce was almost nonexistent until the 1960s. Divorce rates in the United States have had a very strong impact on U.S. cultural changes. The divorce rate in the United States tripled between 1960 and 1990, and it is estimated that 40 percent to 50 percent of children born in the late 1970s and early 1980s would experience the divorce of their parents (Bumpass, 1990).

Cultural changes in the family, in work environments, and in the community had eroded for youth the developmental significance of social institutions other than school. As extended families (many adult family members living together) were replaced by nuclear families, the number and variety of people with whom adolescents closely interacted was systematically reduced. Not only were there fewer grandparents, aunts, uncles, cousins, and siblings, but also there were fewer opportunities and less time for intimate or productive involvements (U.S. House of Representatives, 1975).

One of the most obvious consequences of the evolution of family, work, and community was the steady erosion of the roles of youth. In each case, opportunities for purposeful activity, for meaningful interaction with adults, and for the testing of competencies under real-life conditions had decreased as U.S. culture further postponed the age at which such opportunities become available. Virtually the only arena in which adolescents had a socially recognized and accepted role was in the secondary school; yet this institution never was intended, nor had it been equipped, to meet all of the varied needs of children and youth (Hruska, 1978).

During this period, a growing number of cataclysmic societal changes influenced the causes and outcomes of violence in U.S. schools. Dysfunctional families, substance abuse, changing values of the adolescent subculture, and myriad personal and societal problems influenced the social, emotional, and personal development of young people.

1970s

The growth of illegitimacy — especially in the inner cities — has been linked to escalating violence. In 1970, about 11 percent of births were out of wedlock; by 1991, nearly 30 percent were out of wedlock (Office of Juvenile Justice and Delinquency Prevention, 1991a).

In 1970, the typical U.S. household breadwinner was bringing home the same pay that he would be bringing home 20 years later in 1990 (after inflation is subtracted and amounts are placed in 1990 figures). The family in 1990 had approximately 20 percent more buying power than the family in 1970 because of the increase in two-income households. Birthrates also experienced a decline between 1970 and 1990, dropping from 18.4 births per 1,000 people to 16 per 1,000 people (Office of Juvenile Justice and Delinquency Prevention, 1991b).

In the late 1970s, about 12,500 parents decided that the best way to counter many of the problems that they saw was to institute home schooling; this number was projected to rise to more than 700,000 children being schooled at home by 1995 (U.S. Department of Commerce, Bureau of the Census, 1992).

In the early 1970s, 12 percent of all families were single-parent households; by the mid-1980s, this rate had doubled. In the mid-1990s, 8 million U.S. families are headed by single mothers. Approximately 400,000 of these have incomes of $50,000, and 1.5 million have incomes of $30,000 or more. The median income of female-headed households with children under age 18 is $13,000, compared with $24,000 for male-headed households and $43,000 for dual-earner families (U.S. Department of Commerce, Bureau of the Census, 1992).

One of the few national surveys of school crime was conducted by the National Education Association (Rubel, 1977). This study demonstrates how fear can develop exponentially from harms that actually occur to the chance of the same harms occurring to someone else. The 1970s saw extreme fear of teacher victimization, although the percentage of teacher assaults by pupils ranged from 2.0 percent in 1971 to a high of 3.0 percent in 1973. Most of the teacher assaults that occurred were perpetrated by angry parents or older students who had left the school.

Between 1971 and 1974 (Rubel, 1977), magazine and newspaper articles started to appear across the country dealing with the increased security budgets and increased number of security agents hired to help control school crime. Gallup polls during this three-year period also started to show the impacts of school disturbance. Three of the top five public concerns focused on pupil misbehavior.

In 1975 (Goldstein, Apter, & Harootunian, 1984), a safe school report was released nationally by Senator Birch Bayh's subcommittee to investigate juvenile delinquency. A survey of 750 U.S. school districts had been conducted, and the report found the following increases between 1970 and

1973 (p. 2): 19.5 percent increase in homicides on school grounds, 40.1 percent increase in rapes and attempted rapes, 36.7 percent increase in robberies, 85.3 percent increase in student to student assaults, 77.4 percent increase in student to teacher assaults, 37.5 percent increase in alcohol and drug offenses, and 54.4 percent increase in the number of weapons confiscated on school grounds.

In the 1970s, results of new research contended that crime was not caused solely by harmful social conditions. Experts noted that most low-income youth were law abiding and that even the wealthiest neighborhoods were not crime free. Juvenile justice experts began to focus less on social problems and more on individual motivations for crime (Drowns & Hess, 1990).

In 1972, reform schools in many states had become so large, overcrowded, and understaffed that experts believed these institutions to function more as training schools for future criminals. In 1974, the U.S. Congress passed laws encouraging all states to close their reform schools (Drowns & Hess, 1990).

In the late 1970s, there was strong public outcry for the nation to get tough on juvenile offenders. Many juvenile courts switched back from their caregiver philosophy to more of the punishment philosophy found in adult courts (Drowns & Hess, 1990).

Prior to the 1970s, it had been a common practice for educators to skirt their responsibilities in dealing with problem youth by pushing them out of the educational system. By the decade of the 1970s, however, court decisions tended to stress that all youth had the right to an education and must be dealt with in the educational setting. Youth who had been found delinquent or status offenders could no longer legally be dismissed from school on the recommendation of a teacher or an administrator. School counselors who formerly concerned themselves with academic advising and scheduling had to face the reality of coping with behavioral or emotional problems in their advisement of delinquent youth. It was determined that schools, not reform schools, were the best places to meet the needs of delinquent youth (Cox & Conrad, 1978).

The relationship among education, occupational success, and life satisfaction began to persuade educators to attempt to minimize the number of juveniles who were pushed out or who chose to drop out of the educational system. Educators began to realize that this work would require not only academic and vocational information but also the promotion of psychological and social well-being, moral development, and a sense of direction and purpose for juveniles. It was determined that if educators failed to provide for these concerns, juveniles often had nowhere to turn except to their peers, who may be experiencing similar problems. One result of this alienation from both the family and the educational system is the development of delinquent behavior patterns (Cox & Conrad, 1978).

Data from the FBI and other sources indicated that violence in schools throughout the United States had increased at epidemic rates in the 1970s. Programs aimed at ameliorating the problem of violence and vandalism increased greatly in popularity. Many public schools implemented programs that utilized uniformed police officers, sophisticated alarm systems, tightened security measures, and other preventive activities.

Increases in school property damage and assaults on teachers by students occurred in the late 1970s. School crime remained essentially level, or declined for thefts from teachers and all offenses against students, in the 1970s and 1980s. Junior high schools and schools in large cities were likely to experience more crime against persons than were senior high schools or schools in less urbanized locations (Moles, 1987).

Other reform efforts centered on treatment of those who became delinquent. The educational implications for the treatment of delinquents were most often of two types in the 1970s. One was to establish special institutions to take care of those who required special treatment, in the form of either clinics or some kind of school for rehabilitation. The other was to secure the help of various agencies trying to work with children in serious need in the predelinquent stage. The roles and responsibilities for education pointed toward providing services to assist children who were socially maladjusted and hence potential delinquents; help given through special schools and classes as well as by specialized personnel (Cox & Conrad, 1978).

During the period 1970–73, there was a 77 percent increase in assaults on teachers, an 85 percent increase in assaults on students, a 37 percent increase in robberies of students and teachers, a 40 percent increase in rapes or attempted rapes, an 18 percent increase in homicides, and a 53 percent increase in weapons confiscated from students. Concomitantly, drug and alcohol use on school grounds increased by 37.5 percent and the incidence of dropouts by 11.7 percent (Gottfredson, 1975).

A major problem had developed during the 1920s that persisted into the next six decades. Even with the high incidence of juvenile crime problems, there was little consensus in the clarification of the nature and goals of the activities undertaken to fight these problems. Additionally, very little firm evidence demonstrating the effectiveness of any program in the treatment or prevention of juvenile problems was collected. Although evaluations were sometimes conducted, research on program effectiveness was fragmented, diverse, and sometimes poor quality. An approach would be widely accepted despite sketchy knowledge of its positive effects. Consequently, school anticrime programs were often ill conceived, ineffectively implemented, and poorly managed. The general conclusion to be drawn was that incidents of crime on school campuses were not significantly reduced as a result of any of these programs (Subcommittee to Investigate Juvenile Delinquency, 1977).

Many educators believed that police officials should be brought onto school campuses only in extreme emergencies because the presence of uniformed officers created additional problems and resentments for students (Ianni & Ianni, 1980).

R. Cavan and T. Ferdinand (1975) concluded that juvenile delinquency was demonstrated in three ways in public schools in the 1970s: serious misconduct in and around schools; truancy, both as delinquency and as the open door to other kinds of delinquency; and the day-long idleness of those who dropped out of school before graduation and found it difficult to become incorporated into conventional adult activities such as steady employment.

The 1970s saw extreme concern about the use of illicit drugs by juveniles. It was believed that the behavior patterns that were popularized and institutionalized in the 1960s would continue to pull more and more students into what appeared to be a relevant, youth-oriented drug subculture. A recent high school survey offers information to the contrary. A random selection of high school seniors were surveyed and asked whether they had ever used any type of illicit drug. The following data, classified by year of graduation, report the results of that survey:

These data suggest that illicit drug use by students dropped 14.5 percent between 1975 and 1992, with significant drops since the mid-1980s. During this period alcohol use remained relatively stable, showing a decrease of 2.9 percent.

In January 1975, a grand jury in San Francisco issued a report stating that secondary schools were overwrought with concern for the safety of the students. In December 1977, the U.S. Department of Health, Education, and Welfare released statistics indicating that in a given month, a typical secondary school student had approximately one chance in 9 of having a personal belonging stolen, one chance in 8 of being attacked, and one chance in 200 of being robbed (U.S. Department of Health, Education, and Welfare, 1977).

	Percent Who Used:	
Year of graduation	Illicit drugs	Alcohol
1975	55.2	90.4
1976	58.3	91.9
1977	61.6	92.5
1978	64.1	93.1
1979	65.1	93.0
1980	65.4	93.2
1981	65.6	92.6
1982	64.4	92.8
1983	62.9	92.6
1984	61.6	92.6
1985	60.6	92.2
1986	57.6	91.3
1987	56.6	92.2
1988	53.9	92.0
1989	50.9	90.7
1990	47.9	89.5
1991	44.1	88.0
1992	40.7	87.5

Source: Adapted from U.S. Department of Commerce, 1992, p. 3.

The following is a list of educators' perceptions of factors that contributed to the problems of school violence in the 1970s:

School Factors
  Building size
  Class size
  Dreariness of school building
  Educators unwilling to acknowledge problem
  Expectations of the schools
  Failure of schools to report crimes
  Compulsory attendance regulations
  Ignorance of due process
  Lack of alternatives to suspension
  Lack of parent/educator unity
  Lack of professional unity
  Lack of sufficient commitment to problem
  Lack of teacher/student relations
  Staff hostility, aggressiveness

Staff inadequacy
Whole curriculum

Nonschool Factors
    Bad student attitude
    Boy-girl triangles
    Community responses
    Family feuds
    Lack of community awareness
    Ineffective juvenile justice system
    Lack of multi-cultural understanding
    Lack of coordination of community services
    Lack of parental interest
    News media cause problems
    Parents, community workers confront teachers
    Police handling of students
(Glasser, 1978, p. 331).

Beginning in the 1970s, schools gradually assumed more responsibility for the conduct and welfare of their pupils. To the basic academic and instructional purposes of education, many schools added medical and dental examinations, nutrition concerns, vocational and psychiatric counseling, and vocational training. Schools also developed special curriculums and classes for children with disabilities, while assuming broad policing functions for disruptive children. Only when the disruptions reached extremely serious levels did schools feel compelled to call for police aid (Cernkovich & Denisoff, 1978).

School boards and principals did not like to admit that they could not maintain discipline and that occasional serious delinquencies or crimes occurred in and around schools. Frequently these offenses were of a type that would immediately command police attention if they occurred elsewhere: serious thefts, major vandalism, physical attacks, retaliatory counterattacks by male teachers or principals, and sexually inappropriate behavior of adolescent boys (Cernkovich & Denisoff, 1978).

In 1977 a new term was coined for what many teachers were beginning to feel: "battered teacher syndrome" (Goldstein, Apter, & Harootunian, 1994). The term was used to explain the stress reaction that some teachers experienced as depression, anxiety, headaches, disturbed sleep, and eating disorders. A cause of the stress reaction might have been the failure of many of the sure methods that teachers had depended on. The student population had changed so much as the country moved toward the 1980s that every classroom combined students from many geographical areas and cultural backgrounds.

The national scope and seriousness of youth gangs increased sharply during the late 1970s and early 1980s. Gang violence rose drastically in a number of large cities during this time. Gangs emerged in many mid-sized and smaller cities and in suburban communities across the country at the same time. Youth gangs became more violent and, increasingly, ways for members to engage in illegal money-making activity such as street-level drug trafficking (Moles, 1987).

In the mid-1970s, W. Miller (1975) conducted the first nationwide study of youth gangs. Results of the study found youth gang problems in 50 percent of the nation's large metropolitan areas. The ten cities with the largest gang problems contained about one-half of the gangs. Miller estimated that 300 U.S. cities and towns contained about 2,300 youth gangs composed of nearly 100,000 members. About 3,400 gang-related killings were reported for some 60 cities during a 13-year period ending in 1980.

There has been a continued movement of gangs from urban to suburban areas since this time. Gang members move to suburban and rural areas when police pressure and enforcement increase or to find more lucrative areas for their money-making activities. In addition, in mid-sized and small towns where factories close or businesses fail, unemployment, poverty, and unrest create conditions conducive to gangs (Tursman, 1989).

Many researchers in the 1970s concluded that if for no other reason, the sheer amount of time youth spend in school and in school-related activities cannot help but importantly shape their values, attitudes, and behavior; delinquent or otherwise. Many authorities on youth problems also felt that the school was clearly neither the cause nor the cure for norm-violating behavior among young people. The influence of the school, whatever the direction or extent, was inseparable from the influences of other socializing agencies. Behavioral scientists generally agreed, however, that the school context had the capacity either to help initiate and nurture delinquent behavior or to help prevent and curb it (Cernkovich & Denisoff, 1978).

In 1978 the findings of a landmark school crime study were released in a report titled *Violent Schools — Safe Schools* (Gaustad, 1991). This research was initiated by the U.S. Congress and conducted by the National Institute of Education to determine the frequency and severity of crime in elementary and secondary schools in the United States. The study found that teenagers were more likely to become victims of violence at school than anywhere else. On average, 5,200 secondary school teachers, or 0.5

percent of all secondary school teachers, were physically attacked each month of the period 1970–77.

1980s

In 1983, the National Commission on Excellence in Education issued the first and most influential report on the state of education. Titled *A Nation at Risk*, this report stated that the nation was at a turning point and that significant changes needed to be made in educational systems across the country. During this same year, three more national reports discussing the sorry state of education in the United States were released. All of these reports found the same four primary problems in U.S. education: inadequate emphasis on academic studies, absence of leadership, lack of standards, and poor teaching (Perkinson, 1995).

The 1980s has sometimes been labeled the period of violence and punitiveness toward children (Hyman & Lally, 1980). The 1980s saw severe cuts in educational programs combined with increased reports of juvenile delinquency and child abuse. This period also saw the growing of strong resentment and anger against U.S. youth. Older adults especially began to push for more severe treatment of youth.

Results of a study conducted in 1988 found that the number of schools with serious drug problems had declined considerably from 1980 to 1985. The results showed that student drug use was more problematic than alcohol use before and during school, whereas both alcohol and drug use were problematic after school. The proportion of students attending schools suffering from serious drug problems decreased from about one in four students in 1980–81 to about one in seven students in 1984–85. The most common explanation given for decreases in student alcohol or drug use was changes in a school's discipline policy or increased enforcement of existing policy (Moskowitz & Jones, 1988).

On February 1, 1985, public juvenile facilities nationwide housed 49,322 juveniles, a 1 percent increase from 1983. During 1984 there had been more than one million admissions or discharges from public juvenile facilities. The number of juvenile admissions (521,607) was slightly higher than the number of juvenile discharges (515,301). Thus, 1984 juvenile admissions were 11 times greater than the average daily population of adults who were incarcerated. Females accounted for about 20 percent of these juvenile admissions and discharges (Bureau of Justice Statistics, 1993).

Between 1985 and 1988, adolescents aged 12–15 were about twice as likely as older teens to experience crime in a school building or on school property. About 37 percent of violent crimes and 81 percent of crimes of theft against younger teenagers occurred at school, compared with 17 percent of violent crimes and 39 percent of crimes of theft against older teens. Younger teens were more likely than older ones to be robbed or assaulted at school, but the two age groups experienced similar numbers of robberies and assaults outside of school. Violent crimes against teenagers that took place in school or on school property were much less likely than street crimes to be committed by armed offenders. Violent street crimes against teens were three times as likely as crimes in school buildings to be committed by offenders with weapons (37 percent versus 12 percent) (The National Crime Victimization Survey, 1991).

A survey of youth in custody in 1987 (Bureau of Justice Statistics, 1993) found that an estimated 60.5 percent of the juveniles incarcerated were between the ages of 15 and 17, 12.4 percent were age 14 or younger, and 27 percent were age 18 or older. About 70 percent of the juveniles and young adults did not live with both parents while they were growing up. More than half (54 percent) reported having lived primarily in a single-parent family. Almost 43 percent of the juveniles had been arrested more than five times, with more than 20 percent of them having been arrested more than 10 times. More than 80 percent of the residents reported the prior use of an illegal drug; almost 40 percent of those who had used drugs began doing so before age 12.

Other characteristics suggest that school crime and street crime against teens were similar in severity. Similar proportions of victims of violent crimes were physically attacked in school buildings and on the street. Teen victims of school crimes and street crimes were equally likely to sustain injuries. Although violent crimes on school property were some-what more likely than those on the street to involve physical attacks, the proportions of victims who were injured did not vary (31 percent versus 32 percent). Violent offenders committing crimes in school buildings were more likely than those committing crimes in the street to be under age 21, white, female, and well-known or casual acquaintances of the victim (The National Crime Victimization Survey, 1991).

From 1986 through 1990, the number of delinquency cases disposed of by juvenile courts increased by 10 percent. During this same time, juvenile courts disposed of 31 percent more violent cases, including 64 percent more homicides and 48 percent more aggravated assaults (Snyder, 1993).

Admissions to juvenile facilities rose after 1984, reaching an all-time high in 1990 and with the largest increase in detention. Forty-seven percent of confined juveniles were in detention and in correctional facilities in which the population exceeded the design capacity of the facility. More than half of the detained and incarcerated population in 1991 were held for nonviolent offenses (Parent, 1993).

Standard sentencing was first introduced in 1986. The U.S. Department of Justice issued a study that recommended states adopt standard penalties for all juveniles convicted of crimes. Previously, juvenile courts looked at offenders' personal histories, not their crimes, to determine their sentences; often, this led to discrepancies in the sentences of two juveniles who committed the same crime. Standard sentences were developed to do away with this sentencing problem (Drowns & Hess, 1990).

In a nationally representative sample of public school teachers, 44 percent reported more disruptive classroom behavior in 1986–87 than five years before. Almost one-third indicated that they had seriously considered leaving teaching because of student misbehavior. Teachers estimated that about seven percent of the students they taught were habitual behavior problems and interfered with their teaching. Almost 20 percent of the teachers surveyed indicated that they had been threatened by a student at some time (National School Safety Center, 1992).

Data from the 1987–88 school year revealed more than 2,500 incidents against staff members in New York City. Teachers found that the treatment they received after the crime often constituted additional injury and lengthened their periods of recovery. Teachers who had been victimized reported very casual treatment and response to their attackers, citing that they were ignored, left in offices by themselves, asked to fill out confusing forms without help, unaccompanied to emergency rooms, and generally treated as though they were the criminals rather than the victims (Feder, 1989).

Nationwide, self-reported measures of delinquent behavior indicated an increase in certain violent acts in the late 1980s, especially in aggravated assault and robbery. National victimization surveys also showed that the rate of juvenile victimization for violent offenses had increased during the latter part of the 1980s (Bureau of Justice Statistics, 1993).

According to the Bureau of Justice Statistics, during a 6-month period in 1988–89, more than 400,000 students experienced violent crimes at school, including assault, robbery, and rape. Because of the potential for violence in schools, 430,000 students armed themselves for protection. The need for security systems such as metal detectors, guards, locker searches, restroom monitors, walkie-talkie units, and visitor badges contributed to the students' fear of danger. Weapons came to be classified as any instrument that could cause injury by an assailant. Students frequently carried sharp and pointed objects such as spiked jewelry, razor blades, knives, and brass knuckles to school (Pepperdine University National School Safety Center, 1991).

Juvenile arrests for violent crimes increased 41 percent between 1982 and 1991. In 1991, the juvenile arrest rate for violent offenses reached its highest level in history. In the 10-year period between 1982 and 1991, the number of juvenile arrests for murder increased by 93 percent, and aggravated assault arrests increased by 72 percent (Snyder, 1993). In 1988, new studies found that half of the juveniles held in state detention facilities committed their offenses while under the influence of drugs or alcohol. This evidence opened new challenges for the juvenile justice system (Drowns & Hess, 1990).

A survey (Bureau of Justice Statistics, 1994) of murder cases disposed of in 1988 in the courts of large urban counties offers a different aspect of the examination of juvenile-related crime and victimization. Among murder victims, 3.5 percent were children killed by their parents, and 1.9 percent were parents killed by their children. In murders of persons younger than age 12, the victims' parents accounted for 57 percent of the murderers. For murder victims younger than age 12, death was often preceded by child abuse; in 57 percent of such cases, the assailant had abused the murder victim. Among offspring murder victims who were younger than age 12 before their deaths, 79 percent had suffered abuse by the assailant. Rape or sexual assault preceded the deaths of 6 percent of murder victims younger than age 12.

In 1988 some experts estimated the yearly cost of school vandalism at $5 million. Targets of vandalism included buildings, equipment, and furnishings; other types included painting on walls and property, theft, lavatory damage, driving cars across lawns, and defacing school furniture. Most acts of vandalism were committed by the school's students, and such acts were as prevalent in affluent suburban schools as they were in inner-city schools. It was determined that the typical vandal was a white male about 15 years old (Sadler, 1988).

In 1989, the death penalty for juveniles was reaffirmed in *Stanford v. Kentucky*. In this case, the U.S. Supreme Court held that the death penalty given to a juvenile who was charged and convicted as an adult did not violate the constitutionally guaranteed right against cruel and unusual punishment (Drowns & Hess, 1990).

In 1989, the volume of juvenile admissions and discharges to public correctional facilities was the highest since 1970, totaling more than 1.23 million. Minority youth — blacks, Hispanics, and other races — constituted 60 percent of the juveniles in public custody facilities. The number of females held decreased by 8 percent since 1987. The number of juveniles held for violent personal offenses reversed its decline and showed an increase for the first time since 1983. Between 1987 and 1989, there was an 8 percent increase in the number of juveniles held for committing offenses against persons (Office of Juvenile Justice and Delinquency Prevention, 1991b).

The National Crime Victimization Survey (1991) collected U.S. student responses about the extent of violence in their schools between January and June 1989. An estimated 9 percent of students, aged 12–19, were crime victims in or around their schools during a 6-month period; 2 percent reported experiencing one or more violent crimes, and 7 percent reported at least one property crime. Violent crime is largely composed of simple assaults, involving attacks without weapons and resulting in minor injuries such as cuts or bruises. Violent crimes such as aggravated assaults, robberies, and rapes were also included.

A 1989 survey found that 25 percent of children of divorce saw their fathers at least once a week and 33 percent no more than once a year. In 1990 almost one in five single parents was a male. Generally, father-headed homes fared better economically because men receive higher incomes than women. Boys did especially well, probably because they usually respond better to male authority. Fathers also received more child care assistance from outside sources. The number of single-parent homes and homes in which both parents work continues to increase. Working mothers of school-age children in 1992 comprised 82 percent, compared with 30 percent in 1960 (U.S. Department of Commerce, Bureau of the Census, 1992).

The two-working-parent structure has provided Americans with the highest per capita family income in the nation's history; however, 14.5 percent of Americans live in poverty (U.S. Department of Commerce, Bureau of the Census, 1992). The resultant bipolar socioeconomic structure may mean that curriculums that are relevant to one segment of the population are irrelevant to many other students and their parents. The combination of irrelevant curriculums and children left alone at home with no adult supervision must be considered before other concrete school violence prevention efforts can be initiated.

1990s

Prior to the 1990s, sympathy for children who injured or killed their parents would have been unheard of. Such children were regarded as evil or mentally ill and usually earned the harshest judgments of the public and the courts. This attitude has slowly changed. Children who strike back at abusive parents are drawing more understanding from a public that has awakened to the national nightmare of child abuse. According to the National Center for Prevention of Child Abuse, in 1991 an estimated 2.7 million youngsters were physically, mentally, and sexually assaulted by their parents. Despite the prevalence of abuse, parricide (killing of father, mother, or close relative) remains rare. This disquieting crime accounts for about 2 percent of all homicides, around 300 cases a year. Most of those cases involve teenagers who kill abusive parents. Although the numbers are small, these youngsters are demonstrating a devastating way to end child abuse (Toufexis, 1992).

U.S. culture continues to change in the 1990s. Approximately 85 percent of homes have television sets and video cassette recorders, generating nearly $10 billion in annual videotape rentals in a market that did not exist 20 years ago. The impact of television and entertainment violence continues to generate debate while access and availability increase (Toufexis, 1992).

More than three-quarters of all women in prison in 1991 had children. An estimated 25,700 female inmates had more than 56,000 children younger than age 18. Male inmates were slightly less likely to have children, with 64 percent having any children and 56 percent having children younger than age 18. Black (69 percent) and Hispanic (72 percent) female inmates were more likely than white (62 percent) women to have children younger than age 18. Black women were slightly more likely than other women to have lived with their young children before entering prison. Among inmates with children younger than age 18, 25 percent of the women but nearly 90 percent of the men said that their children were living with the other parent. More than one-third of white female inmates reported one or more of their children living with their fathers, compared with one-fourth of Hispanic women and less than one-fifth of black women. Regardless of race, the children's grandparents were the most common single category of caregivers: 57 percent of black mothers, 55 percent of Hispanic mothers, and 41 percent of white mothers. Nearly 10 percent of the women reported that their children were in a foster home, agency, or other institution (Bureau of Justice Statistics, 1994).

A National Crime Victimization Survey report found that in 1991 an estimated 21.6 million students aged 12–19 lived in the United States. Results of the survey revealed that an estimated 9 percent of students were crime victims in or around their schools. Overall victimization rates were similar for males and females. Two percent reported experiencing one or more violent crimes, and 7 percent reported at least one property crime. Violent crime consisted largely of simple assaults. Nine percent of public school students and 36 percent of private school students reported that drugs were impossible to obtain at school (Bastian & Taylor, 1991).

Fifteen percent of the students said their schools had gangs, and 16 percent claimed that students had attacked or threatened teachers at their schools. Of 700 cities responding to a survey covering August and September 1992, 38 percent said there had been a noticeable increase in school violence during the past five years. The largest cities were also the most likely to report increasing violence during the past five years (The National Crime Victimization Survey, 1991).

A University of Michigan study (Violence in Schools, 1993) reported that 9 percent of eighth graders carried a gun, knife, or club to school at least once a month. In all, an estimated 270,000 guns were brought to school every day. Inner-city schools have started adding drive-by shooting drills to traditional fire drills. Schools have fenced in their campuses, installed metal detectors, and instituted locker searches and student shake-downs. The Los Angeles School Board decided in October 1993 to put its armed plainclothes security officers in uniforms and to add nightsticks to their weaponry.

The actual number of teachers who are victims of violence nationwide is not known, but is probably underreported. Many teachers are injured attempting to either break up student fights or halt robberies; however, not all teacher injuries are caused by students. Psychic violence against teach-ers — intimidation and verbal abuse — is unmeasured but nevertheless present in the classroom. This kind of violence causes many teachers who are new to the system and who do not have much invested to give up and quit (Foley, 1990).

Nearly 20 percent of the student respondents to a survey in 1991 reported that they had carried a weapon during the previous school year. Boys were more likely to have weapons than girls, and Hispanic and black males more likely than white males. An estimated 71 weapon-carrying incidents occurred per 100 students per month. Knives and razors were carried more often than clubs or firearms (Weapon-carrying, 1991).

In 1993 it was reported that 135,000 students on average brought guns to school each day (Hill & Hill, 1994). During that same year, 20 percent of students in a national survey expressed fear and concern about the number of guns in their schools; 31 percent of their parents feared that their children would become victims of hand-gun assaults on their way to school.

The middle 1990s have found the suburbs providing fertile ground for juvenile gang movement from the inner city (Hill & Hill, 1994). Schools in nonurban areas are starting to see gangs develop after only one student transfers from an urban school with a gang problem. Schools are also seeing younger and younger students involved in such groups.

Another problem that schools are experiencing in the 1990s is random selection for public aggression (Hill & Hill, 1994). Thirty documented cases of a person entering a school building and beginning to shoot have occurred since 1984. Most often the offender is an estranged spouse of an employee, an angry parent, or a disgruntled former employee, but an increasing number are random shootings by people with no connections to the schools.

Supreme Court decisions combined with an increase in the nature of gang and drug activity continued to change the juvenile court system from a "kiddie court" to a mirror of the adult system. The marked changes in the nature of juvenile crimes have probably had the largest impact on this movement. During the past several decades (especially during the 1980s and 1990s), the crimes committed by youth have become more serious and more violent (Pope, 1995).

Since the 1980s and early 1990s, juvenile courts have taken more retributive postures, similar to those in the adult system. The most pronounced sign of this change can be found in the significant increase in the use and nature of waiver decisions that transfer custody of youth to adult courts; this practice has included the lowering of the age at which waiver is permissible (dropping to 14 years in many states) (Pope, 1995). Such change in practice has resulted from the belief that there is no adequate excuse for the serious and violent acts committed by modern youth.

Some believe that the juvenile justice system in the 1990s is becoming a repository for every pathology that affects the modern dysfunctional family. Encountering battered babies as well as babies born drug addicted, HIV positive, or suffering from fetal alcohol syndrome, the courts are also dealing with child sexual abuse, abandonment, violent custody battles, and termination of parental rights. Additionally, the courts decide the fates of children who vandalize, rape, rob, sell drugs, and commit murder (Horowitz, 1992).

Ironically, the philosophy of the juvenile justice system in protecting society's children and changing the behavior of delinquents has changed little since its inception. Despite the increase in the violence in juvenile crime, the juvenile justice system operates within a structure designed when the worst crimes children committed were shoplifting or stealing hubcaps. The system still attempts to balance the needs of the community with those of the child; this approach seeks to change behavior rather than to punish (Pope, 1995).

Most observers believe that the system remains more concerned with the criminal than with the crime and that rehabilitation is still the main objective. Critics find fault with the system because it rarely asks whether rehabilitation is possible for someone who has grown into adolescence without any type of moral grounding, education, or hope for the future (Pope, 1995).

Some make the case that the problems facing modern youth are no different from the problems of 5, 10, or 20 years ago. Others state that there are numerous modern and unique problems facing adolescents. Ten years ago, the major fears of young people centered on boyfriend or girlfriend problems, finding a date for the prom, or getting into trouble for coming home too late. In the 1990s, the fears deal with more universal problems such as global warming, unemployment, or becoming a victim of a drive-by shooting. In the past, the issues of dating and sex caused stress in that teenagers worried about finding cars for Friday night dates and, at the most, worried about a pregnancy. The modern era has produced the additional fears of assault, date rape, and AIDS. Twenty years ago young adults, for the most part, were following their parents' advice and waiting until they married to have sex. In the 1990s, many children are having sex as soon as their age reaches double digits (Nilsen & Donelson, 1993).

It appears that political candidates typically overstate how much better a job educators did 30 or 40 years ago than they are doing in the 1990s. For many people it is difficult not to believe that there are major problems in public schools that were not typical in the past. The growing power and violence of gangs, the extensive availability of drugs and guns, crack babies now of school age, and the large number of adolescents who are having babies are but a few of the problems that teachers, principals, and other school staff are taking into account as they go about their task of educating U.S. youth (Rosen, 1994).

The amount of alcohol or other drug abuse is debatable at any time. Many observers believe that drug use continues to rise in drastic proportions, while statistics indicate a constant and stable amount of use by teenagers and decreases in many age groups (Nilsen & Donelson, 1993).

Often there is confusion about the definition of school violence; therefore, efforts to fight school violence must involve caution by educators. Violence is not always a matter of shootings or assaults; it can be sexual harassment, intimidation, and abuse (bullying) between students. Administrators must be cautious of quick-fix programs such as metal detectors and armed guards, which are effective band-aids for school problems. There will still be a need for long-term solutions. Schools should acknowledge programs that work, and administrators must implement changes that seem to work (S. Splittgerber-Wise, personal communication, March 12, 1994).

A recent Gallup poll (1993) of 400 parents across the country reported the number one concern (78 percent of respondents) as drugs in schools. Violence in general was the second concern (68 percent of respondents). Interestingly enough, the quality of teachers (59 percent of respondents) and poor curriculum (50 percent of respondents) were of lesser concern.

One view that attempted to predict events in the 1990s is found in the document *Turning Points: Preparing American Youth for the 21st Century*, produced by the Carnegie Council on Adolescent Development (1989, p. 1) and the Carnegie Corporation of New York: "As a nation we face a paradox of our own making. We have created an economy that seeks literate, technically trained and committed workers, while simultaneously we produce many young men and women who are semi-literate or functionally illiterate, unable to think critically and untrained in technical skills, hampered by high-risk lifestyles, and alienated from the social mainstream."

A second view was offered by Senator Christopher Dodd, chair of the Senate Subcommittee on Children and Families, in the introduction to the Young Americans Act (Dodd, 1986):

Far too many Americans today are growing up at risk. The majority of poor Americans are children, with one out of every four children under the age of six now living in poverty. We rank at the bottom of 20 industrialized nations with respect to infant mortality rates. Children whose families cannot find housing are now overcrowding shelters for runaways. And homeless children and families now constitute 30% of those without shelter. This year one out of every four students will leave high school without a diploma. In some of our inner cities 75% of all young people will have dropped out of school before they turn 16 years old. . . . We do strategic planning for every other area of critical importance. We have long-term plans for the military. . . . We have long-term plans for our nation's highways, bridges, and tunnels, because they provide the infrastructure for our democracy. . . . Children are the future security for this country and the future infrastructure for our democracy. So it is about time we worked on a comprehensive plan for the 63 million Americans who are children. The changing student population is a product of the above cited societal changes. While children are watching more television, functional illiteracy and technological illiteracy are increasing. More disturbing are patterns of negative behavior that are starting younger (i.e., drug use, sex, alcohol, and etc.). Many feel this pattern is due to the many problems that students face: physiological changes, more exposure to violence, shifts in family relations, (i.e., divorce/one parent families). There is also more pressure to grow up quickly, pressure to do well in school, pressure to engage in sex and drugs, and pressure to misbehave in general (Allen, Splittgerber, & Manning, 1993)

Another source of concern is the possible negative impact of life during nonschool hours. Children often have no place to go and very little of a constructive nature to do. About 40 percent of adolescents' waking hours are discretionary, not committed to specific activities such as eating, attending school, or going to work. Many adolescents spend virtually all of this discretionary time without companionship or supervision from responsible adults. Much of this time is spent alone, with peers, or with adults who may serve as negative role models or who may exploit the young person (Task Force on Youth Development and Community Programs, 1992).

Students' reasons for seeking counseling have changed dramatically in the past 20 years, from problems with puberty, concern over appearance, and dating to problems with incest, divorcing parents, alcohol or drug abuse, and fears over safety (Nilsen & Donelson, 1993).

The statistics reported by the popular press state that each year, 700,000 students drop out of high school, costing the nation more than $240 billion in lost earnings and foregone taxes. Dropout rates for black youth and Hispanic youth are two times greater than the dropout rate for white students. One-third of high school graduates possess marginal basic skills and often cannot order two items from a lunch menu and then calculate how much change they are owed after paying a cashier three dollars (Donmoyer & Kos, 1994).

Although modern teenagers are not the first in history facing difficult decisions, certainly few would argue that these teens have a special set of problems unique to their age and modern culture (Nilsen & Donelson, 1993).

In the twentieth century, the current major cause of concern by professionals, parents, and children is the impact that school violence has on the children and the school. With no feeling of safety, children cannot learn to their fullest capacities. In extreme cases where 80 percent of a teacher's time is spent on discipline, the teacher has severely limited time to teach. School violence affects what is taught, how and where teaching occurs, and who is taught. Violence is a norm in society, and it has become so in the classroom (Shepherd & Ragan, 1992).

SUMMARY

Teacher surveys conducted in the early 1960s found discipline and school disturbance to be of minimal concern. A study conducted in the late 1960s would find occurrences of crimes never before seen in schools: rapes, homicides, drugs, and serious physical assaults on teachers. There would be debate whether there was a 7,100 percent increase in the number of teachers assaulted during this decade, but all agreed that "school violence" would now be the appropriate term for what was occurring in U.S. classrooms.

Fear of crime would come to be the major focus of the 1970s. The tidal wave of crime that had begun in the late 1960s would cause people to continue to question their safety in their homes, neighborhoods, and, increasingly, their schools. Reports continued to question the competence of teachers and the effectiveness of schooling. Negative societal changes such as illegitimacy, divorce, and poverty would cause many to once again look to education to solve these problems.

National reports in the 1980s would discuss the sorry state of U.S. education, centering on the problems of inadequate emphasis on academic studies, absence of leadership, lack of standards, and poor teaching. In society there was a return to harsh treatment of juveniles for their negative conduct. Drugs would be the primary focus of school violence and problems in the 1980s. The war on drugs intitiated in the United States would carry over into the schools, and locker and student searches would be daily occurrences. These changes would cause juvenile correctional institutions to become dangerously overcrowded and the adult court dockets to be flooded with the large numbers of youth being waved to adult court for drug use and violent acts.

The 1990s are seeing any and every type of violent act being committed in the classrooms or on school campuses across the United States. Drugs, sexual assaults, and gangs are inundating schools across the country. The get-tough attitude of the 1980s continues to serve as the catalyst for most of the treatment of youth and juvenile delinquency. National crime surveys continue to show the drastic increases in random violence and the decrease in the age of perpetrators.

Events in the late 1990s will probably continue to rock the U.S. public and their ideas of schools and the educational process. This time will probably continue to see a deterioration in many societal areas, and education will be asked once again to solve problems that it did not create in environments that it cannot control. When education cannot provide satisfactory solutions to these problems, the quality of education and teachers will once again be critized and questioned.

7

Possible Solutions to School Disturbance in the United States

There are numerous suggestions for solving the present state of violence and disruption in U.S. schools, many concentrating on the process of education itself. Major increases must be made in high school and college completion rates in the United States. Thus, money must be earmarked for those activities that will directly improve high school and college graduation rates (Hodgkinson, 1990).

There is increased awareness of the central role that schools can play in preventing delinquency. Every youngster spends a considerable amount of time in school, and therefore many delinquent acts are committed within the school setting. Researchers have frequently noted that weak commitments to educational achievement and attachments to the school culture combined with association with delinquent peers appear more closely related to delinquency than do variables in family, community, or social structure. Educators have proposed, therefore, that the most effective school-based prevention efforts would be to increase students' experiences of academic success, stimulate student-to-student and student-to-teacher relationships, encourage commitments to school culture, and stimulate attachments between students and nondelinquent peers (Hawkins & Wall, 1980).

THREE PROPOSED SOLUTIONS
TO SCHOOL VIOLENCE

Theorists have developed six general building blocks for preventing student-to-student violence: a shared system of beliefs and values, a vision of respect, explicit policies, a holistic plan of staff development, district statements of policy, and the use of learned strategies. Policies and legislation that protect school employees, provide teacher training in conflict resolution, help in the creation of a school culture and sense of community, foster the development of an emergency school plan, and establish reasonable precautions to protect school staff are ways to reach the goal of reducing school violence. Educators, when assaulted, should pursue every legal means possible against the assailant and force the attacker to face the consequences of violent behavior while providing the victim full support (Curcio & First, 1993).

One of the greatest problems contributing to school violence is lack of parental involvement, but there are many strategies for increasing parental involvement in efforts to fight that violence. Parent representatives can be added to school safety committees and school improvement teams. Meetings scheduled at breakfast, at lunch, or in the evening could make parent attendance more feasible. A copy of the school's discipline code can be sent to all parents. A communication system utilizing strategies such as a parent telephone network, calling parents at work, or sending brief notes home could be effective. Administrators can recruit parents and students to paint and clean up during summer months and can use parent volunteers to patrol schools during the year. School districts could provide transportation for parents to attend meetings. Teachers can develop parent-student homework assignments. Law enforcement agencies could invite parents to participate in school crime watch programs (Greenbaum, Gonzales, & Ackley, 1989).

There are also many educational strategies for violence prevention. Teachers can teach students about the nature and extent of violence in society, possibly preventing hate crimes with discussions to help students develop positive attitudes toward minority groups. Schools can use existing courses to teach safety topics and increase awareness of the damaging effects of sexual harassment and sexual assault; such courses would teach about specific laws that affect juveniles and the consequences of breaking those laws. Through videos and newspaper reports, teachers can discuss and show students the lethal impact of guns and the legal implications of carrying or using guns. Schools can videotape television news stories that describe incidents involving guns and form discussion groups about them (Southeastern Regional Vision in Education, 1993).

Additional educational strategies include teaching problem-solving skills and gang avoidance. Students can be taught that anger is an acceptable feeling but that aggression is not an acceptable action. Schools can offer assistance in finding jobs and teaching social skills (Southeastern Regional Vision in Education, 1993).

Teen Court

A relatively new but potentially vital idea in handling student disputes and arguments is teen court, a dispositional alternative in which first-time juvenile offenders are tried by a jury of their peers. Since the first teen court opened at Odessa, Texas, in 1983, teen courts have appeared in Arizona, Colorado, Oregon, California, Michigan, New York, Georgia, Indiana, and Florida. Teen courts have had encouraging results. In Odessa, 15 percent of juvenile traffic offenders and 1 percent of other offenders recidivate. The failure rate for the Montgomery County, Indiana, teen court is between 10 and 15 percent, while that of Gila County, Arizona, is less than 12 percent (Collins, 1992).

Teen courts receive referrals from juvenile courts. While not designed to determine guilt or innocence, teen courts function as a dispositional alternative. Adjudications are handled by a district court; teen jurors hear the details of each case and recommend a constructive sentence. Every participant in teen court is between the ages of 14 and 17, except for the judge, who is usually a retiree from the district court. The jurors listen to a case, then adjourn to the deliberation room for discussion. A foreperson is elected, and the case is discussed until a unanimous decision has been reached. After the jurors return to court, the bailiff instructs the defendant to face the jury. The foreperson reads the constructive sentence to the defendant, who is then issued the completed jury form and told to meet with the teen court coordinator to finalize sentencing arrangements. If the jury sentence is unacceptable to the judge, jury deliberations must begin again (Collins, 1992).

Researchers state that there are essential elements of a school climate that must be developed to help handle the problems of school violence: Schools must be physically safe and emotionally secure environments with curriculum programs that are academically effective and developmentally appropriate. Students need emotional and psychological growth through diversity, self-exploration, meaningful participation in school and community, positive social interaction, and physical activity, among other competencies (Allen, Splittgerber, & Manning, 1993).

Children must feel like they are valued and cared for. If they are not valued by family, church, community, and school, then children often look to be valued by the street gangs or other negative peers (B. Nesbit, personal communication, March 12, 1994).

In dealing with criminal justice issues, police officers should work as part of a community-based team that includes the social, educational, and judicial resources of a locality. The public education system should be part of the community-based team because it provides an ideal base of operation from which police officers can deliver education, prevention, intervention, and enforcement services to the community. Educational law enforcement (a relatively new idea) builds on the value of community-based policing. It asserts that an emphasis on early intervention and the encouragement of citizenship values in youth provide the greatest long-term investment in funding community police services. Police officers serving as mentors work one on one with students to gain the trust of the youth community. Educational law officers also seek to help students develop higher self-esteem by achieving goals and projects. In addition, young people receive formal instruction designed to improve decision-making skills. Educational law enforcement relies on restrictive enforcement activities as a last resort (Johnsen, 1992).

Community, home, and school must have a strong presence in a child's life. If any of these key components are weak, the remaining components must pick up the slack. There must be approaches such as school safety plans, conflict resolution instruction, peer counseling, and peer mediation that can help strengthen each of these components (B. Nielsen, personal communication, March 12, 1994).

Some basic problems often prevent many school efforts from working. For example, the school often has no idea about the background of a transfer student, who could have been expelled in another state for a serious violent act. In addition, when a child arrives at school on Monday morning, teachers have no idea about the problems that the child or child's family might have encountered during the weekend. If students are arrested over the weekend (even for a violent act), they are often released to parents to return to school. There is no requirement to inform the school of the problem, and administrators often know nothing until violence occurs in school (B. Nielsen, personal communication, March 12, 1994).

School Safety Plans

A relatively new strategy for fighting school violence is the development of school safety plans. The basic components of these plans are to identify the problem, determine how each school will prevent this problem, decide what will happen if a problem occurs, resolve how the school will handle the media, and agree what the school will do after the problem is solved.

Numerous suggestions for other activities that schools can pursue include the following:

provide student supervision (all hours),

call parents often,

develop strong discipline policies,

involve police when needed,

communicate with everyone,

develop emergency response teams,

teach law-related education courses to students,

establish a program for students to skip grades and catch up,

practice emergency skills,

make counseling available for all after an incident,

use block scheduling,

lower the number of students in the halls at any given time,

limit changes between rooms,

determine problem areas in school,

develop student leadership,

establish parent-student swap programs,

make parents pick up report cards,

survey as many people as possible,

provide a crime line so that students can report problems anonymously by telephone, and

target troublesome grades: sixth, seventh, eighth, and ninth. (B. Nesbit, personal communication, March 12, 1994).

The South Carolina State Department of Education has proposed four policy recommendations for the prevention of school violence. In the planning stage, schools must have an emergency preparedness plan, which would be activated immediately when a school disturbance occurs.

The second recommendation deals with staff development. In this stage all teachers, counselors, aides, and administrators would be trained to recognize signs of trouble and to use intervention strategies and prescribed response patterns when a crime or disturbance occurs. The third recommendation focuses on community involvement, which is crucial in preventing any criminal activity in the school setting. Finally, sensitization to students is crucial. Research indicates that many crimes in schools stem from students' lack of self-esteem and confidence (South Carolina Department of Education, 1993).

Through staff development, teachers must be taught to understand the signs of impending conflict, including a sudden shift in the clustering of students, a sudden clustering of rival groups, unusual movement of a group from its normal territory, or a group of students appearing at an activity that they normally would not attend. Other indicators are isolated racial or intergroup fights, an incident or disorder in the community at large, the sudden appearance of underground publications complaining of inequality in disciplinary treatment, a disproportionate number of disciplinary actions, a sudden increase in organized demands from students, complaints about a lack of grievance procedures, warnings from nonteaching staff, increase in graffiti at school, and parents withdrawing their children from school. School administrators can reduce violence and develop a safer school climate by being highly visible, establishing and enforcing written rules, actively involving parents, eliminating graffiti, keeping security personnel moving through the building, fencing the campus, keeping the campus grounds clean, and shortening periods between classes. Administrators should keep staff members informed about potential problems, deal with rumors quickly and responsibly, isolate combatants, and deal with threats as if they were acts of violence (Brooks, 1993).

Violence has become more frequent at school athletic events and in school recreation centers. Such violence often involves shooting, physical fights, and brawls between rival fans and teams. The threat of violence has become so prevalent that school officials and coaches have developed contingency plans such as bullet drills, in which students are told that, in the event of gunfire, they are to lie face down in the center of the field, classroom, or gymnasium until the all-clear is given. Violence near high schools has also prompted tighter security at games and special events. Spectators are sometimes searched, and police presence at games has been increased. Primary components of a strategy to curb violence at recreational activities include faculty preparation, an effective communication network, crisis prevention, adult supervision, school/law enforcement partnerships, and active student participation. Effective athletic event management must go beyond intervention and supervision, however. Violence prevention programs that clearly identify behavioral expectations and rules for special events must be established. Discussion about proper and improper roles and behaviors for students, coaches, athletes, and school staff must occur. An antiviolence curriculum must be implemented to utilize peer mediation and conflict resolution programs to assist students with defusing incidents before they become major problems (Brooks, 1993).

There are at least three components to a school's effective control or suppression strategy. The first component provides for the development of a school gang code, with guidelines specifying appropriate responses by teachers and staff to different kinds of gang behavior, including a mechanism for dealing with serious gang delinquency. The second component calls for the application of these rules and regulations within a context of positive relationships and open communication by school personnel with parents, community agencies, and students. The third component is to clearly distinguish between gang and nongang activity so as not to exaggerate the scope of the problem (Schmitze, 1993). Schools must have a plan for student supervision before and after school because school personnel often leave the school grounds, but the students do not. Communities must fight boredom by establishing programs that involve students. Students who are involved in extracurricular activities (for example, Junior Reserve Officer's Training Corps, band) are much less likely to become involved in crime (B. Nesbit, personal communication, March 12, 1994).

Efforts such as those just described must be combined with positive after-school, weekend, and holiday activities, positive adult role models, school-based community services and activities, and police-driven efforts to reach out to children before problems emerge (Majority Staff of the Senate Judiciary Committee, 1994).

Some obstacles to the development of effective school safety plans are denial by school officials that a problem exists and insufficient understanding of the problem. There also is a reluctance by many educational systems to view school security as a profession (Trump, 1993).

All efforts must have community support. Schools must have everyone's support for any effort to have a chance at succeeding (S. Splittgerber-Wise, personal communication, March 12, 1994).

Security Programs

Schools across the United States are experimenting with many different types of security programs. One such program is conducted by the National Crisis Prevention Institute of Brookfield, Wisconsin, which uses a team of experts to train teachers and administrators to defuse disruptive or assaultive students. The teachers learn the telltale signs of a potentially violent situation and the proper verbal and nonverbal responses to calm the situation before it escalates (Brooks, 1993).

The United Federation of Teachers in New York has provided personal alarms to teachers in elementary schools in Brooklyn. These devices are very accessible for teachers and unnoticed by students. Pulling the alarm's pin activates a loud noise to alert security personnel (Brooks, 1993).

Modern school planners and architects have committed themselves to the general objective of personalizing space to give each person the perception of ownership. This principle translates to the identification of territories within the school campus. Responsibility for the general supervision and care of these newly assigned territories goes with ownership — a fundamental concept of space management for crime prevention. Significant school problem areas that require space-management design consideration are school grounds, parking lots, locker rooms, corridors, restrooms, and classrooms. Problems on school grounds often stem from poorly defined campus borders, undifferentiated campus areas, isolated areas, and poorly located bus loading areas. Parking lot problems typically include poor planning (that is, conflict with the neighborhood, poor placement, and landscaping). Problems associated with lockers and locker rooms include the assignment of more than one student to a locker, locker design and color, and isolation. Corridor problems include blind spots due to poor planning and class scheduling that promote confusion and congestion. Restroom security problems typically stem from location. Other problems are multipurpose classroom use and isolation (Crowe, 1991).

RECENT EFFORTS

There are many ways to improve school safety. Metal detectors are one obvious but minimal solution. The first priority is to gain student support of school safety and safety education. Police can assist in this effort by establishing substations in schools and by identifying qualified officers to become certified teachers in classes on issues such as conflict management, enforcement of truancy rules, and parent involvement. A school can combat violence by fighting juvenile delinquency during school hours as well as after and by using older students to serve as school patrols while serving as role models. Schools can work with local law enforcement to develop school safety plans that are comprehensive and that provide an environment in which students can learn and teachers can educate (C. Austin, personal communication, March 12, 1994).

Many factors will affect the issue of police in the schools over the next decade: taxpayer support for educational services, qualified public school teachers in the state, the number of minority students attending public schools, public concern over violent crime in public schools, and the presence of dysfunctional families. If police presence is required, the measures likely to be taken include restricting students convicted of violent crimes from attending public schools, requiring schools to develop comprehensive school safety plans, and conducting mandatory drug abuse prevention and gang prevention programs in the school curriculum (Schmitze, 1993).

Violence in schools is not a new problem, but the number of serious offenses is a new phenomenon. As a result, school administrators are taking an inventory of school security measures or are attempting to develop violence prevention programs for their schools or districts. Developing a violence prevention plan requires a careful examination of what is already being done in the areas of substance abuse prevention, teen pregnancy, and habitual truancy; causes are similar, if not the same, and solutions overlap. Solutions require keeping factual perspectives about families, communities, and the successes and failures of schools (Rosen, 1994).

Public schools, especially middle schools, are potentially the best community resources for the prevention of and early intervention into youth gang problems. The peak recruitment period for gang members is probably between the fifth and eighth grades, when youth are doing poorly in class and are in danger of dropping out. Most schools, overwhelmed by other concerns, tend to ignore or deny the problem (Schmitze, 1993).

When circumstances force schools to acknowledge youth gang problems in and around schools, the first reaction is to increase school security. Probation and youth service agencies may be invited to develop gang prevention programs in the schools; otherwise, school programs receive little restructuring, including the targeting of high-risk gang youth for special supervision and remedial education (Schmitze, 1993).

Sometimes probation officers have established in schools special outreach programs that involve parent education, family counseling, and referral. Special antigang curriculums for children in the early elementary grades are usually taught by representatives of outside agencies. Although evidence suggests that these curricular efforts succeed in changing attitudes of youth about gangs, it is not clear that the behavior of youth who are already gang members is also changed (Schmitze, 1993).

In the fall of 1993, a citizens' panel in Washington, D.C. (a coalition of groups that included the American Medical Association and the National Parent-Teacher Association), presented U.S. Attorney General Janet Reno with a series of recommendations aimed at curbing violence on television between the hours of 6 A.M. and 10 P.M. These citizens felt that a major cause of school violence and juvenile delinquency was exposure to television violence. Attorney General Reno informed a Senate panel that government action was needed if the entertainment industry did not take it upon itself to reduce television violence. This movement resulted in the federal government and the Federal Communications Commission attempting to persuade the entertainment industry to voluntarily limit violence. The threat of regulation was suggested if the entertainment industry failed to examine the violence problem and propose plans to reduce violent programs (Brooks, 1993).

A study conducted in 1994 sought to examine the effect on violent behavior of neutralizations (not realizing the full impact of one's violent actions upon others) regarding violence. Data indicated that only a small percentage of adolescents generally approve of violence or express indifference to violence. A large percentage of adolescents, however, accept neutralization, which calls for justifying the use of violence in specific situations. Both cross-sectional and longitudinal data suggested that the acceptance of these neutralizations contributed to violent behavior. Furthermore, the effect of neutralizations on violence was conditioned by certain variables: Neutralization is most likely to lead to violent behavior among those who disapprove of violence and associate with delinquent peers. Most of this neutralization occurs from watching television (Agnew, 1994).

In April 1993, President Clinton submitted a proposal for *Goals 2000* (1993), which sought to spearhead a national effort toward the solution of school violence. This act established voluntary national standards such as content standards, which are broad descriptions of the skills students should acquire in English, mathematics, and other subject areas, and opportunity-to-learn standards, which are criteria for determining whether students have access to qualified teachers and necessary textbooks and learning.

The proposal called for a national council to approve voluntary national standards for schools. States would submit their proposed standards to this panel. A similar national board would identify essential occupational skills and create a voluntary system of standards assessments and certification procedures for job training programs. The six national education goals adopted in 1990 by President Bush and the nation's governors would be written into federal law. The goals range from ensuring that children start school healthy and ready to learn, to raising the high school graduation rate to 90 percent by the year 2000.

The National Education Goals Panel would be established in federal law. The council would continue to monitor progress toward meeting goals and would work to generate public support for reforms. A $393 million fund would be established from which states could receive grants to develop plans for meeting the national goals (*Goals 2000*, 1993).

This initiative is planned to build on what works for schools. It proposes higher academic standards, better training for teachers, using new technology to facilitate learning, improving school safety, and making parents equal partners in the education process. *Goals 2000* is believed to be the first critical step in President Clinton's effort to create a system of lifelong learning by serving as a framework for additional education legislation. In 1994, Congress passed the School-to-Work Opportunities Act, which included occupational skill standards (Riley, 1994).

In 1995 the U.S. Department of Education began working on the safety of public buildings by giving $18 million in federal school security grants under the Safe Schools Act to 19 different school districts around the United States (Kilian, 1995). During the same year, the ultimate safe school was announced to exist in Texas (Applebome, 1995): Townview Magnet Center, a $41 million school in Dallas, had 37 surveillance cameras, six metal detectors, and five full-time police officers. It is reported to be the school of the future, with its security-conscious configuration based on the principles of crime prevention through environmental design.

In the mid-1990s, metal detectors became fixtures of many U.S. schools. The legal right of school officials to use these metal detectors and other means to search students for weapons continues to be questioned. Appellate courts across the country are continuing to uphold this right for school officials, as long as there is a reasonable basis for any individualized searching of students (Fegelman, 1996).

In 1996, two solutions were proposed that are more reminiscent of the past than ones looking toward the future. During his first term of office, President Clinton made numerous speeches stating his belief that violence, in any form, must be taken out of U.S. schools. In February

1996, he spoke in Long Beach, California, to bring public attention to the first district in the United States to require students to wear uniforms. He also announced that he had directed the Department of Education to distribute manuals to all 16,000 U.S. school districts outlining how they could do the same (Pertman, 1996).

Before 1996, federal laws dealing with crime were designed to fight one specific type of organized crime: the "Mafia." The Racketeer Influenced and Corrupt Organization statute was designed to fight organized crime, although legislators at the time viewed street gangs as cliques of young criminals engaged in small crimes. They did not see the potential that gangs had to become organized syndicates engaged in serious crimes such as murder, weapons and drug trafficking, illegal gambling, and robbery. To fill this void in federal law, Senator Dianne Feinstein authored the Federal Gang Violence Act of 1996, which doubles the penalties (under U.S. sentencing guidelines) for any member of an organized criminal street gang who commits a federal crime. Interestingly, it also makes a felony the recruiting of minors to join a criminal street gang and the wearing of body armor by a gang member during the commission of a federal offense (Feinstein, 1996).

A final possible solution to school violence is potentially sad but possibly prophetic of what may lie in the future of many schools. Tutt Middle School in Augusta, Georgia, decided to build an eight-foot wall around the school to protect its grounds from stray gunfire from a nearby apartment complex (Spaid, 1996). This wall may be symbolic of how many schools across the United States are going to have to take extreme measures to insulate themselves and their students from an increasingly violent society. Although the wall may keep outside societal violence from entering the school grounds, it may not stop the violence inside from entering society.

8

Continuing Issues in
School Disturbance

A disciplined environment was a desired goal of educators even before the problems of drugs and violence disrupted schools. Maintaining a disciplined environment conducive to learning does not necessarily mean adopting tough policies to keep students silent in their seats; it means principals and teachers working together to develop appropriate curricular and instructional techniques in support of one main goal: to improve students' academic performance in the contexts of appropriate personal and social development. The key seems to be that schools need to create an atmosphere in which students and teachers are engaged in learning and in which misbehavior is dealt with quickly, firmly, fairly, and consistently. Most important, a learning environment requires a caring attitude that shapes staff-student relationships. Changes in classroom organization and management may also be necessary to maintain such an atmosphere. In some cases, these changes might involve alternative settings in which disruptive students receive special attention, counseling, and remediation.

ANALYSIS OF SCHOOL DISTURBANCE
IN THE UNITED STATES

A review of the literature related to school disturbance, vandalism, misbehavior, and violence in U.S. schools from the inception of the public school movement to the present day yields several interesting findings.

The U.S. school system has been an institution of social change; however, while the school seeks to effect change through increased education to produce expanded economic opportunity, it also serves as a reliable reflection of whatever is positive and negative in the social setting. If a social behavior such as violence can be found in society, therefore, it is certain to be present to some degree in the schools of the United States.

Social Transitions

The United States was experiencing many different societal transitions in the first part of the twentieth century. These transitions had serious effects on society and social institutions such as families, schools, and communities.

The 1920s have been looked upon as the bountiful days of prosperity and growth. During this decade, society first began to question the ways of the past and to seek more enjoyment in their lives. A new generation of young adults would lay the foundation for later generations of teenagers who would question adult, parental, and institutional authority. The youth explosion of the Roaring Twenties shocked society with outrageous fads and controversial beliefs and attitudes.

Prohibition made hidden drinking the fad of the day. Women began to smoke and drink with the casual ease that men enjoyed. More young adult males owned cars and changed forever the concept of courting into dating. Dating itself has traditionally been a catalyst for change in teenage practices and attitudes.

The casual way in which many Americans treated Prohibition was one of the first times that it became socially acceptable to break the law with impunity. Some social critics have viewed the rise of organized crime and the popularization of gangsters in this period as the beginning of social violence in the United States.

Another transition that occurred in families was seen between 1929 and the late 1950s. Middle-class parents began to be more tolerant with their child-rearing duties. At the same time, the lower class began to push their children toward greater emulation and acceptance of middle-class goals.

The stock market crash of 1929 would end this wonderful period and drastically affect the country with the economic depression of the 1930s. A period of self-examination of the social and economic system followed.

World War II would also cause great upheaval for the country. It brought about heavy demands on U.S. social and economic institutions and increased the responsibilities of the schools. Teaching became a position of importance and status in the culture of the United States.

At the end of World War II, people began to realize that a new era had begun in which much of what had been done in the past would no longer be adequate. It would now be necessary for people to learn more and to learn faster than ever before.

During this time, the population grew rapidly, resulting in significant shifts to suburban living. Overcrowded classrooms and shortages of well-qualified teachers were common. Many shortages were encountered because the country was not prepared for the returning veterans, who came back to a new world with new inventions, new behaviors, and new values.

The 1950s continued this movement and came to be known as the time of suburbia, when families moved into single-family houses and had backyard cookouts and picnics. The flight of the middle class to the suburbs brought about a concentration of parents who sought status for their children through education and who demanded better schools. A noted development during this time was the increase in kindergartens. More families started to experience the reality of both parents working, which placed more children in the care of nonfamily members.

Not since the colonial period had neighbors had such an impact on child behavior as in the neighborhoods of the 1950s. Neighbors talked to the children, sometimes actually controlling behavior. Neighborhoods were homogeneous and therefore influenced children with similar values and attitudes. The 1960s would see the first movements in society away from homogeneous neighborhoods to heterogeneous neighborhoods.

During the 1960s the concept of the traditional neighborhood changed drastically. Because of societal upheaval and crime, people began to interact less frequently with their neighbors and became more isolated. Children lost the societal control of the neighborhood and began to look elsewhere for guidance in development of behavior and attitudes.

The 1960s were characterized by upheaval and change. The Civil Rights movement, student protests, the crusade for minority rights, the women's movement, and the Vietnam War protests exposed people to problems and situations that were difficult to face. It appeared to many that the concepts behind the book *Future Shock* had become the reality. The national response to this upheaval was often to fight fire with fire. Nightly television news broadcasts offered views of police fighting protesters with dogs, fire hoses, and riot gear. This violent treatment of segments of society caused some of these people to fight back with more violence. Campus riots, assassinations, sit-ins, and the burning of buildings increased public fear and panic.

The Vietnam War provoked an escalation of armed involvement by the government and an increasingly hostile response by many critics of the war. U.S. citizens were accustomed to fighting and supporting wars that they considered just and honorable. Television cameras began sending back footage of what was occurring and the atrocities that were being committed in the name of war.

The educational system continued to come under fire, with accusations that it was no longer shaping the values and beliefs of children and that there was racism in schools. There was some support for education found in new research being conducted, showing that a child's achievement and behavior in school were affected more by resources in the home than by the school.

A major domestic transition that began in the 1960s and has continued into the 1990s is the increased incidence of divorce. The divorce rate has tripled in the United States in this 30-year period; it is estimated that the divorce rate in the 1990s may affect as many as 75 percent of marriages.

The changes of the 1960s forced schools to assume an even greater share of the burden of the socialization of children. One problem area that pointed to the need for socialization was that of illegitimacy. The growth of illegitimacy has been linked to the increase in societal violence beginning in the 1970s. Out-of-wedlock births tripled between 1970 and 1990. The social implications of these births are significant because the babies are likely to have problems: The mothers are often very young, and the children and their parents often strain the resources of the welfare system.

In the 1970s, there was a resurgence of people deciding to teach their children at home. There was also a dramatic increase in single-parent households, which tripled by 1990. The number of homes in which both parents worked continued to increase, almost tripling by 1990.

The 1980s was one of the most prosperous periods in U.S. history. The two-income family structure provided the highest per capita family income in the nation's history. Conversely, during this same period, a growing portion of the population was found to be living in poverty and unemployment. U.S. society became almost a bipolar system in which citizens were either prosperous or destitute, with the gap between rich and poor expanding rather than decreasing.

The 1990s have become a contradictory time in U.S. history. The contradictions are no more apparent than in perceptions toward violence and crime. Never before has there been as much concern for the causes of crime and for visualizing the criminal as a victim. At the same time, there has been a strong conservative movement that has pushed for a get-tough attitude toward criminals and more sympathy for the victims of criminal activity.

The research on the impact of society, dysfunctional families, and poverty on criminal behavior that came from the 1980s began to gain support in the early 1990s. In early 1995, however, this support was being muted by the strong lock-them-up attitude seen in governmental policy and court decisions.

U.S. culture continues to change. The impact of technology has offered the public the option of carrying out almost every activity — shopping, eating, and being entertained — from their living-room chairs. With technology comes new opportunities and problems that most of the United States probably has not even considered.

By 1995, the United States had become the most diverse country in the world. This diversity encompasses race, nationality, religious beliefs, and political opinions. Many have said that the 1990s will soon emulate the 1960s in societal uproar and change.

School Disturbance Characteristics

Young people have participated in criminal behavior to some degree throughout recorded history. School disturbances began in the United States as soon as the first schools were built. Throughout history, as soon as children could learn to walk and talk, they learned obscene language and antisocial behavior. Children were treated as little adults and were expected to act in the same way adults did (drinking, deviant behavior, and sexual activity). It was not until the seventeenth century that the concept of childhood grew to alter the public views of the deviant acts of children. The behaviors that previously had been seen as normal then became unique problems.

An important finding in an examination of the history of school disturbance is that the first violence in U.S. schools was abusive treatment of children by their teachers. Teachers were often expected to use physical discipline with their students. Whipping was considered a teaching aid, and public whipping and flogging were very common.

The colonial era in America saw the same types of discipline being used in schools, with students being tied to whipping posts and beaten. Much of this type of discipline was justified in part by Scripture, which emphasized sparing the rod and spoiling the child. The principles of obedience, submission to authority, hard work, modesty, and chastity were emphasized to students.

Life during this era was dominated by a network of three major social institutions: family, church, and community. The family was to raise children to respect the law and authority; the church was to oversee not only family discipline but also adult behavior; and the members of the community were to supervise each other to detect and correct the first signs of deviancy.

The seventeenth century saw the first compulsory school law, demonstrating the belief that education was the most important aspect of youth development. The "Old Deluder Satan" law emphasized the belief that children had to become educated so that they could read the Bible and avoid the clutches of Satan.

The eighteenth century saw the United States increase in population and become more diversified. Immigration and migration within the country brought more adults to towns and more children to U.S. schools. This change brought people with a wide range of abilities, backgrounds, and aspirations, all of which had to be accommodated by public education.

Until the formation of the first juvenile court in the United States in 1899, there had never been a distinct legal category known as juvenile delinquency. The first definitions dealt with rebelliousness, disobedience, sledding on the Sabbath, or playing ball on public streets.

The nineteenth century found people exhibiting extreme fright and pessimism over delinquent behavior among youth. Many felt that youth were rebelling against the harsh treatment of the past and that the use of barbarous punishment had to be stopped. This century saw discipline problems as a daily occurrence in schools. Poor discipline at school was almost always felt to represent a lack of family discipline. School discipline during this period involved schoolmasters delivering blows with canes or rulers, slapping with hands, boxing ears, and forcing students to kneel on peas or triangular blocks of wood.

The older colonial practice of placing unruly or neglected children in homes of neighbors was no longer possible within the impersonal cities; therefore, houses of refuge and reform schools were established. The concept of "parens patriae" (state acting in place of the parent) became the new philosophy of the time and allowed the government to step in whenever it felt it was necessary to control children.

The last half of the nineteenth century was marked by more immigrants, more urban growth, and more social instability. All of these conditions negatively affected children and their schooling. Immigrants were seen as causing most of the problems facing the country and, therefore, became the objects of social derision.

The beginning of the twentieth century found teachers believing that the most serious behaviors they found in their students were transgressions against authority, dishonesty, immorality, violations of the rules, lack of orderliness, and lack of application to school work. The problems facing schools from the early 1900s to the late 1920s were values of music, art, dancing, and recreational activities for students. The typical school disturbance that was documented in the late 1920s and early 1930s was truancy, which was brought about mainly by the Great Depression. The 1930s found the number one criminal activity committed by children to be vagrancy. The Great Depression developed a large under class whose children would simply roam the streets, often becoming involved in crime. Although street crime was an increasing problem, the most reported school disturbances in the 1940s seemed less serious: The main problems dealt with talking in class, chewing gum, making inappropriate noises, and running in the hallways.

The decade of the 1950s saw the emergence of a serious school dropout problem. The most widely reported school disturbances during this period were stealing, temper outbursts, and masturbation. Gangs also developed in the mid-1950s, causing the first efforts at internal security measures for schools.

The 1960s found school buildings being vandalized, equipment defaced and destroyed, and property stolen. This activity caused a change in the philosophy of dealing with children, with offering children most of the same rights adults had in legal protection and punishments.

The decade of the 1960s brought the first media attention to school disturbance in the United States. Most of this activity began on college campuses and moved down to public education. There were massive increases in violent crime on elementary and secondary school campuses between 1964 and 1968. These incidents caused much fear and concern in the U.S. public. School safety plans would first be developed in the late 1960s.

By the early 1970s, virtually all schools of any size had instituted some type of security in response to violent student behavior. Police also first became involved in school security during this time. Police liaison programs developed across the country.

Increases in juvenile crime continued through the 1980s. Largely because of the national war on drugs, the 1980s were full of concern over drug use by students. Communications media attempted to demonstrate that drug use was rampant in the 1980s and that stricter efforts must be found to eradicate drug use and abuse in the youth subculture.

Surveys conducted during these times continued to demonstrate that drug use was not on the increase. Illicit drug use by students continued to decrease between 1975 and 1995, while student use of alcohol has stayed at a very high and stable rate.

The 1980s and 1990s saw the juvenile court system and the U.S. public taking a more retributive posture against younger transgressors. The juvenile court system of the 1990s has to deal with battered babies, with sexually abused children, and with children who murder their parents. The system still attempts to balance the needs of the community with those of the child.

A major concern in the 1990s has been the impact of school violence on students. Learning is compromised if students must be overly concerned with their safety. Teachers cannot teach as effectively if they must spend the majority of their time disciplining their classes. Juveniles still account for a staggering amount of the violent crime in the United States. In the 1990s, more children are reporting that they either take a gun to school for protection or miss school out of fear for their safety.

Public fear of school violence has spurred the development of security systems in schools, including metal detectors, uniformed guards, locker searches, restroom monitors, walkie-talkie units, and visitor control. It is often said that these preventive security actions have increased student fear and negative public perception more than actual school violence.

Teachers continue to report that the most serious problems that they face in the 1990s are lack of parent involvement and student apathy. Possession of guns and drive-by shootings often do not make survey results list.

On the issue of violence, two areas that are being reported more by teachers and students are areas that are not often discussed in the media: sexual harassment and bullying. These activities are reported more frequently than shootings and muggings. Many feel that these two events can do just as much damage to student self-concept as a lead pipe could do to someone's head.

In striking contrast, studies continue to find that the people actually involved in school disturbances (teachers and students) do not report the same massive increases that the media continues to project in the 1990s. Surveys continue to find that most teachers and students feel safe in their schools and that very few have ever been victimized. Only a small percentage of teachers and students believe that school violence has increased to any significant level in the last several years.

CONCLUSIONS

In the area of violence reduction, solid research on the effects of different strategies is sparse; however, according to available evidence, coordinated school and community efforts seem promising. Within schools it seems clear that the best way to reduce youth violence is by creating an atmosphere that encourages students to focus their energies on learning. Firm, fair, and consistently applied student behavior standards play a part here.

Another major conclusion drawn from an examination of the historical aspects of school disturbance is that public schools in the United States are doing a more effective job in the 1990s of dealing with all of society's children than they have done previously. The professional behavior of teachers and administrators is at high levels of quality. Even with the pervasive problems faced by education in the 1990s, there is still strong evidence that the game has not yet been lost.

Evidence for this conclusion is found in the most recent national survey of public views on experiences with the quality of the U.S. educational system and the extent of school disturbance. The Metropolitan Life Survey of the American Teacher was conducted by Louis Harris and Associates for the Metropolitan Life Insurance Company during April and May 1994. The survey included two sample groups: public school students and parents with at least one child in public school. Both groups were selected to be nationally representative samples.

The findings of this survey and other research related to school violence do not support the widely held belief that schools are on the verge of destruction, that the majority of parents have lost faith in the U.S. educational system, or that most students go to school in constant fear. Some of the positive results contained in this survey relating the attitudes of parents and students are summarized in this chapter.

Most public school students (78 percent) and parents (76 percent) are generally satisfied with their public schools. Most believe their school provides a safe and secure environment as well as a high-quality education. A majority of students have never been victims of violence and have never been physically hurt while in or around school. Most students have not experienced more serious incidents such as threats with a knife (81 percent have had no experiences) or a gun (82 percent have had no experiences). A majority of parents and students believe that their schools provide safe and secure environments in the school buildings. Students generally believe that teachers and students get along (78 percent); very few (3 percent) think they do not get along well at all. In seeming to care for students, a majority of parents and students assess the teachers in their schools as excellent or good. A majority of parents (67 percent) believe relations between teachers and parents are good or excellent (Harris, 1995).

Môst students do not worry about their physical safety going to and from school. A majority of students say the hallways, classrooms, and other public areas in their schools are clean and well kept. In general, students say their schools have taken a wide variety of measures to stop or reduce violence. Most schools have implemented disciplinary codes to help stop or reduce violence; only 14 percent of students say their school has not done this (Harris, 1995).

There is also evidence that many problems that may affect the amount of school disturbance in the country have very little do with school. Instead, these problems center on communication between parents and their children. For example, almost half (47 percent) of students do not talk to their parents about problems or disagreements with other students because they think adults do not understand their problems; one-third (29 percent) say their parents cannot help, and nearly one-fifth (17 percent) say their parents are uninterested or too busy (Harris, 1995).

Many parents worry to some extent about their child's safety while in school or going to and from school. Students do not worry to the same extent about their own safety, and they often underestimate the extent to which their parents worry. Students and parents who worry about safety in or around school most often cite weapons as their most serious concern (18 percent and 16 percent, respectively). This concern is greatest among high school students (20 percent) and their parents (26 percent) (Harris, 1995).

Parents and students have considerably different views about how various environmental issues affect their schools. Parents (71 percent) more often view factors such as overcrowded classrooms and the mass media as contributing to school violence, but only one-half of all students (51 percent) concur. One in ten parents of a high school student says he or she is most worried about drive-by shootings; only 1 percent of high school students mention drive-by shootings (Harris, 1995).

Differences in perceptions between parents and students seem to be very common. Parents say they are involved in their child's school life to a greater extent than students believe. At least half of all students believe their parents never exchange notes with a teacher or school official (58 percent) and never attend meetings of parents' groups such as the PTA (51 percent). In contrast, fewer than one-third of parents say they never have these kinds of contacts (Harris, 1995).

One disturbing difference between parents and school students related to their opinions about the threat or use of weapons. While parents are in nearly universal agreement that using knives or firing guns (98 percent) and threatening someone with a weapon (99 percent) are violent incidents, a lesser proportion of students consider these events violent (93 percent and 92 percent, respectively). Most parents believe that verbal insults, threats to students, threats to teachers, and stealing are violent incidents. Students are less likely to consider these behaviors violent (Harris, 1995).

Another factor that must be considered in the context of school disturbance is the continued need in the United States for a separate juvenile justice system. It appears that the continuing increase in juvenile violence in schools and on the streets has caused the juvenile system to move closer to the adult system. The lines separating the two court systems are frequently blurred in many states, where more juveniles are being tried as adults (Pope, 1995).

The twenty-first century will probably still see a separate juvenile justice system. The major reasons for this continuance are not the need for effectiveness of a juvenile system but rather the tradition of having one and the problems that would be caused in dismantling the system. The juvenile court of the next decade will probably be different from what it is in the 1990s. The court of the future will be more punitive as a reaction to the public demands for get-tough policies, resulting in more juveniles being waived to adult courts, thus receiving adult punishments (Pope, 1995).

If present trends continue, the juvenile court of the future will deal with more minorities, who will be placed in secure public facilities while whites will be placed in diversion programs in private facilities. Demographics will play some role in this because present trends show the white birthrate decreasing and the minority birthrate drastically increasing (Pope, 1995).

Social and school disturbances have been shown to relate to the socioeconomic status of young people. In the contemporary school setting, these young people are usually described as being at risk. Economics will continue to influence at-risk populations. The past decade has seen the erosion of many industrial jobs and entry-level positions. The United States has seen the growth of a large service-based economy with lower wages and unskilled labor. These changes have placed the under class in a relatively disadvantaged, even hopeless, position. Living in this isolated fashion often produces children who must be more concerned with survival than with education and self-improvement. The present trends do not indicate any positive changes for the near future; these children will become the clients of the future juvenile justice system (Pope, 1995).

In the twenty-first century, there will probably be a continued interest in developing a fair and equitable juvenile justice system. Many of the problems of juvenile delinquency cannot be solved by this system. Solutions must be developed before a child enters the juvenile justice system. This is true in the 1990s, and will continue to be so in the future. Only by attending to social and economic problems that force children into the system can the United States hope to have an impact on this problem. There is very little evidence that this will be accomplished in the near future (Pope, 1995).

Schools have typically mirrored the problems of the greater society. The United States has had some evidence of juvenile delinquency and school disturbance since the inception of a formal school. It appears that school disturbance has paralleled violence and crime in society throughout history. The country has tried almost everything to fight school disturbance and juvenile delinquency, with little or no success.

The three major social institutions (family, community, and school) have evidenced shortcomings in the care of children at one time or another. As one area became weak, the other two have had to compensate for the weak component. In the 1990s, schools are expected to assume even greater responsibility, as families and society tended not to satisfy the needs of the young people of the United States. Schools maintain that they are doing the best they can with what they have. Schools are (and have always been) expected to solve problems that they did not create and cannot control.

RECOMMENDATIONS FOR THE FUTURE

Recommendations for future efforts can be divided into four categories: recommendations for the larger society, recommendations for parents, recommendations for schools, and recommendations for further research and investigation.

Three recommendations for society center on informed decision making and proper involvement. First, there has been a lack of research on school disturbance and a tendency toward exaggeration of the problem. Research and factual information would result in an informed concern shown by the U.S. population instead of panic, fear, loss of support, and accusations. Second, individual citizens can make a difference by becoming involved in their schools, regardless of whether they have school-age children. Third, social institutions must continue to generate meaningful activities for youth. It is a very strongly supported belief that there would be less violence in schools and in society if young people had more positive activities in which to participate.

Two recommendations for parents center on responsibilities and opportunities. First, parents need to increase their involvement in their children's schools and ensure that their children know and understand the reasons for their involvement. If they are to succeed, students must feel that they have support from their families. Second, parents need to know what involvements their children have, whether school activity, peers, or neighborhood associations.

Nine recommendations for schools cover intellectual, physical, and psychological concerns.

1. Teachers need to be more accessible to students; students must feel comfortable in talking with their teachers and principals about personal and school-related problems.

2. Schools must target certain groups for special prevention efforts: students who have been victims of violence, are minorities, or of a lower socioeconomic status.

3. Students cannot be treated like numbers; they must receive as much individual attention as possible.

4. There must be an increase in student understanding of the impact of violence and the long-lasting consequences it can have on their lives and the lives of others.

5. Increasing student success is an idea that continues to need addressing. Students who do not achieve in school (getting mostly Cs, Ds, and Fs), and who have been victims of violent incidents at some time in their school lives are more frequently involved in all types of confrontational behavior.

6. Schools must offer a disciplined environment. Tracking generally leads to discipline problems for students in low-ability groups; it would seem that elimination of this process would help. Smaller schools, self-contained classes, and teacher involvement beyond the classroom seem to contribute to a sense of caring that will carry over to the students.

7. In many instances alternative schools can communicate a caring attitude and markedly improve behavior for some students.

8. Student suspension appears to not be a very successful disciplinary measure; in-school alternatives seem to be better solutions for less serious offenses.

9. It appears that principals who focus on instructional leadership and interpersonal relationships and who share planning with teachers are successful in

reducing discipline problems as well as increasing the level of student achievement.

Six recommendations for scholarly research and investigation center on the problem of school disturbance and its effects on students awareness.

1. There needs to be continued study of the relationship between drug use and school violence.
2. There needs to be study of the effect of improved curriculums on school disturbance.
3. There needs to be study of the effect that school atmosphere and teacher attitudes have on school disturbance.
4. There needs to be continued study to determine what efforts can be made by the larger society to assist schools in being more effective, rather than what the schools can do to assist the larger society.
5. There needs to be study to determine procedures for schools to inform the larger society of their school disturbance problems while soliciting support and not invoking panic.
6. There needs to be continued study of ways to improve communication among teachers, students, and parents.

As teachers and principals in the nation's schools strive to attain this sixth goal, research will be needed to provide more insight into the causes of drug use and violence afflicting so many U.S. youth and the means to prevent them. The roots of these ills may be deeply imbedded in society, but schools can be very well positioned to reduce their incidence and their effects on learning. By being armed with an understanding of the complex linkages among the factors that put children at risk, by focusing on the related protective factors that may shelter children from these risks, and by drawing on strong family and community involvement, U.S. schools can become the healthy learning environments that compose a strong defense against drug use and juvenile violence.

Bibliography

Addicott, I. D. (1958). *Teachers guide to constructive classroom control*. San Francisco: Howard Chandler.

Agnew, R. (1994). The techniques of neutralization and violence. *Criminology, 32*(4), 555–568.

Allen, H. A., Splittgerber, F. L., & Manning, M. L. (1993). *Teaching and learning in the middle level school*. New York: Macmillan.

Altman, J., & Ziporyn, M. (1967). *Born to raise hell*. New York: Grove Press.

Applebome, P. (1995, February 20). For the ultimate safe school, eyes turn to Dallas. *The New York Times*, p. B11.

Ash, R. (1972). *Social movements in America*. Chicago: Markham Publishing.

Baker, K., & Rubel, R. (1980). *Violence and crime in the schools*. Lexington, MA: Lexington Books, D. C. Heath.

Bandura, A., & Walters, R. H. (1963). *Social learning and personality development*. New York: Holt, Rinehart and Winston.

Barnes, H. E. (1972). *The story of punishment* (2nd ed.). Montclair, NJ: Patterson Smith.

Bastian, L., & Taylor, B. (1991). *School crime: A national crime victimization survey report*. Washington, DC: U.S. Department of Justice, Office of Justice Programs, Bureau of Justice Statistics.

Berger, K. S. (1994). *The developing person through lifespan*. New York: Holt, Rinehart and Winston.

Bronfenbrenner, U. (1958). *Socialization and social class though time and space: Readings in social psychology*. New York: Holt, Rinehart and Winston.

Brooks, B. D. (1993). *School safety*. Washington, DC: U.S. Department of Justice, Office of Justice Programs, National Institute of Justice.

Bumpass, L. (1990). What's happening to the American family? Interactions between demographic and institutional change. *Demography, 27,* 483–493.

Bureau of Justice Statistics. (1994). *Murder in families*. Washington, DC: U.S. Department of Justice, Office of Justice Programs.

Bureau of Justice Statistics. (1993). *Special analysis*. Washington, DC: U.S. Department of Justice, Office of Justice Programs.

Bureau of Justice Statistics. (1991). *Special report: Women in prison*. Washington, DC: U.S. Department of Justice, Office of Justice Programs.

Burgan, L., & Rubel, R. (1980). Public school security: Yesterday, today and tomorrow. *Contemporary Education, 52,* 34–39.

Butler, N. (1910). *Education in the United States: A series of monographs*. New York: American Book.

Butts, R. F., & Cremin, L. A. (1953). *History of education in American culture*. New York: Holt, Rinehart and Winston.

Carnegie Council on Adolescent Development. (1989). *Turning points: Preparing American youth for the 21st century*. New York: Author.

Carper, J. (1995). *School and the social order*. Unpublished manuscript.

Cavan, R., & Ferdinand, T. (1975). *Juvenile delinquency*. New York: J. B. Lippincott.

Cernkovich, S., & Denisoff, R. (1978). *Value orientations and delinquency: A theoretical synthesis in school crime and disruption: Prevention models*. Washington, DC: U.S. Government Printing Office.

Chambliss, W., & Ryther, T. (1975). *Sociology: The discipline and its direction*. New York: McGraw-Hill.

The charters and general laws of the colony and province of Massachusetts Bay. (1814). Boston.

Chesler, M., Franklin, J., & Guskin, A. (1969). *The development of alternative responses to interracial and intergeneration conflict in secondary schools*. Ann Arbor: University of Michigan, Center for Research on the Utilization of Scientific Knowledge.

CNN Gallup Poll: The Gallup Organization 1993 survey of 400 parents. (1994, October 2). *USA Today*, p. A1.

Cohen, A., Lindesmith, A., & Schuessler, K. (Eds.). (1956). *The Sutherland papers*. Bloomington: University of Indiana Press.

Cohen, S. (1968). Politics of vandalism. *The Nation, 46,* 83–87.

Coleman, J. (1966). *School statistics*. Washington, DC: U.S. Department of Health, Education and Welfare.

Collins, J. (1992). Jury trial by a jury of teen peers. *Insight, 38,* 14–16.

Counts, G. S. (1934). *The social foundations of education*. New York: Charles Scribner's Sons.

Cox, S., & Conrad, J. (1978). *Juvenile justice: A guide to practice and theory.* Dubuque, IA: William C. Brown.

Cremin, L. A. (1970). *American education: The colonial experience 1607–1783.* New York: Harper & Row.

Cremin, L. A. (1961). *The transformation of the school: Progressivism in American education 1876–1957.* New York: Vintage Books.

Crews, G. A., Montgomery, R. H., & Garris, W. R. (1996). *Faces of violence in America.* Needham Heights, MA: Simon & Schuster.

Crowe, T. D. (1991). Safer school by design. *Security Management, 35,* 81–86.

Cubberley, E. P. (1962). *Public education in the United States: A study and interpretation of American educational history.* Cambridge: The Riverside Press.

Cubberley, E. P. (1934). *Public education in the United States.* New York: Houghton Mifflin.

Curcio, J. L., & First, P. F. (1993). *Violence in the schools: How to proactively prevent and defuse it.* Newbury Park, CA: Sage Publications.

Decker, D., & Groth, G. (1983). An interview with William M. Gaines. *The Comics Journal,* 67–72.

Dodd, C. (1986). *Introduction of the Young Americans Act.* Washington, DC: U.S. Government Printing Office.

Donmoyer, R., & Kos, R. (Eds.). (1993). *At-risk students: Portraits, policies, programs, and practices.* New York: State University of New York.

Douglass, A. A. (1940). *The American school system: A survey of the principles and practices of education.* New York: Farrar and Rinehart.

Drowns, R., & Hess, K. (1990). *Juvenile justice.* New York: West Publishing.

Elkind, D. (1984). *All grown up and no place to go: Teenagers in crisis.* Reading, MA: Addison Wesley.

Feder, J. (1989). Crime's aftermath. *School Safety* (National Institute of Justice), 26–29.

Federal Bureau of Investigation. (1973). *Uniform crime reports for the United States — 1972.* Washington, DC: U.S. Department of Justice.

Fegelman, A. (1996, February 27). School gun check upheld. *Chicago Tribune,* p. 1.

Feinstein, D. *The Federal Gang Violence Act of 1996.* (1996). Washington, DC: U.S. Government Printing Office.

Fife, B. (1992). *Desegregation in American schools: Comparative intervention strategies.* New York: Praeger Publishing.

Foley, D. (1990, May). Danger: School zone. *Teacher Magazine,* 57–63.

Garrin, L., & Furman, W. (1989). Age differences in adolescents' perception of their peer group. *Developmental Psychology, 25,* 825–834.

Gaustad, J. (1991). *Schools respond to gangs and violence: Oregon school study council, 34*(9).

Glasser, W. (1978). Disorders in our schools: Causes and remedies. *Phi Delta Kappan, 59,* 331–333.

Goals 2000: Educate America Act. (1991). Washington, DC: U.S. Government Printing Office.

Goldstein, A., Apter, B., & Harootunian, B. (1984). *School violence.* Englewood Cliffs, NJ: Prentice Hall.

Good, H. G., & Teller, J. D. (1973). *A history of American education* (3rd ed.). New York: Macmillan.

Goodlad, J. (1967). *The educational program to 1980 and beyond: Implication for education of prospective changes in society.* Denver, CO: Bredford-Robinson Printing.

Gottfredson, G. D. (1975). Organizing crime: A classificatory scheme based on offense transitions. *Journal of Criminal Justice,* 331–333.

Graham, H., & Gurr, T. (1969). *Violence in America: Historical and comparative perspectives.* New York: Bantam Books.

Greenbaum, T., Gonzales, R., & Ackley, J. (1989). *Student views.* Sacramento: California State Department of Education.

Haan, A. (1961). *Elementary school curriculum: Theory and research.* Boston, MA: Allyn and Bacon.

Harris, L. (1995). *Metropolitan Life survey of the American teacher, 1993–1995: Violence in America's public schools.* New York: Author.

Haskell, M., & Yablonsky, L. (1978). *Crime and delinquency.* Chicago: Rand McNally.

Hawkins, J. D., & Wall, J. (1980). *Alternative education: Exploring the delinquency prevention potential.* Washington, DC: U.S. Government Printing Office.

Hill, M., & Hill, F. (1994). *Creating safe schools: What principals can do.* Thousand Oaks, CA: Corwin Press.

Hirschi, T. (1969). *Causes of delinquency.* Berkeley: University of California Press.

Hirschi, T., & Hindelang, M. (1977). Intelligence and delinquency: A revisionist review. *American Sociological Review, 42,* 571–586.

Hodgkinson, H. (1990). *South Carolina: The state and its educational system.* Columbia, SC: Institute for Educational Leadership Inc., Center for Demographic Policy.

Horowitz, D. (1992, February). How the juvenile justice system is letting kids get away with murder. *New York,* 18–27.

Hruska, J. (1978). *The obsolescence of adolescence in school crime and disruption: Prevention models.* Washington, DC: U.S. Government Printing Office.

Hyman, I. A., & Lally, D. M. (1980). Corporal punishment in American education: A historical and contemporary dilemma. In J. R. Cryan (Ed.), *Corporal punishment in the schools: Its use is abuse.* New York: Harper & Row.

Ianni, F. A., & Ianni, E. (1980). *What can schools do about violence: Today's education.* Washington, DC: National Education Association.

Illich, I. (1971). *De-schooling society*. New York: Harper & Row.

Johnsen, D. P. (1992). *Educational law enforcement: Community-oriented polic-ing in the public schools*. New York: Harper & Row.

Joint Special Committee. (1863). *Report of the committee*. Hartford, CT: Author.

Kaestle, C. F. (1983). *Pillars of the republic: Common school and American soci-ety, 1780–1860*. New York: Hill and Wang.

Kellogg, A. M. (1893). *School management: A practical guide for the teacher in the schoolroom*. New York: E. L. Kellogg.

Kerner, O. (1968). *Report of National Advisory Commission on Civil Disorders*. New York: Bantam Books.

Kilian, M. (1995, April 23). City to get large safe schools grant. *Chicago Tribune*, p. 2C.

Kobetz, R. (1971). *The police role and juvenile delinquency*. Gaithersburg, MD: International Association of Chiefs of Police.

Lazerson, M. (Ed.). (1987). *American education in the twentieth century: A docu-mentary history*. New York: Teachers College Press.

Majority Staff of the Senate Judiciary Committee. (1994, April). *Catalogue of hope: Crime prevention programs for at-risk children*. Washington, DC: Author.

Matza, D. (1964). *Delinquency and drift*. New York: John Wiley and Sons.

McDermott, J. (1980). High anxiety: Fear of crime in secondary schools. *Contemporary Education, 52*, 3–8.

Merton, R. (1938). Social structure and anomie. *American Sociological Review, 3*, 574–576.

Miller, W. (1975). *Violence by youth gangs and youth groups as a crime problem in major American cities*. Washington, DC: U.S. Government Printing Office.

Moles, O. (1987). *Trends in student misconduct: The 70's and 80's*. Washington, DC: U.S. Department of Justice, Office of Justice Programs, National Institute of Justice.

Moskowitz, J., & Jones, R. (1988). Alcohol and drug problems in the schools: Results of a national survey of school administrators. *Journal of Studies on Alcohol, 49*(4), 299–305.

National Association of School Psychologists. (1993). *National Association of School Psychologists*. Washington, DC: National Association of School Psychologists.

National Center for Education Statistics. (1994). Washington, DC: U.S. Department of Education.

National Center for Education Statistics. (1993). *Safe schools study*. Washington, DC: Author.

National Center for Education Statistics. (1992). *1991 Statistics*. Washington, DC: Author.

National Center for Education Statistics. (1974). *Safe schools study*. Washington, DC: Author.

The National Crime Victimization Survey. (1991). *National Crime Victim Survey for 1991* (NCJ-131645). Washington, DC: U.S. Government Printing Office.

National School Safety Center. (1992, September). *Working on a game plan for safety* (School safety update). Malibu, CA: Author.

New Jersey Juvenile Delinquency Commission. (1972). Programmed for social class: Tracking in high school. In K. Polk & W. Schafer (Eds.), *School and delinquency* (p. 110). Englewood Cliffs, NJ: Prentice Hall.

Newman, J. (1980). From past of future: School violence in a broad view. *Contemporary Education, 52,* 40.

Nilsen, A., & Donelson, K. (1993). *Literature for today's young adults* (4th ed.). New York: Harper Collins College Publishers.

Office of Juvenile Justice and Delinquency Prevention. (1994). Washington, DC: U.S. Department of Justice, Office of Justice Programs.

Office of Juvenile Justice and Delinquency Prevention (1991a). *National juvenile custody trends: 1978–1989.* Washington, DC: U.S. Department of Justice, Office of Justice Programs.

Office of Juvenile Justice and Delinquency Prevention. (1991b). *OJJDP update on statistics.* Washington, DC: U.S. Department of Justice, Office of Justice Programs.

Oliver, W. A. (1953). Teachers' education beliefs vs. their classroom practices. *Journal of Education Research, 47,* 47–55.

Owen, E. (1991). *Trends in academic progress: Achievement of American students.* Washington, DC: National Center for Education Statistics.

Parent, D. (1993, April). *Conditions of confinement: A study to evaluate conditions in juvenile detention and corrections facilities.* Washington, DC: U.S. Department of Justice, Office of Justice Programs, Office of Juvenile Justice and Delinquency Prevention.

Pepperdine University National School Safety Center. (1991). *Gangs in schools: Breaking up is hard to do.* Sacramento, CA: U.S. Department of Justice.

Perkinson, H. J. (1995). *The imperfect panacea* (4th ed.). New York: McGraw-Hill.

Pertman, A. (1996, February 25). Clinton touts school uniforms. *Boston Globe,* p. 25.

Philadelphia House of Refuge. (1835). *Report of the Committee of the Board of Managers.* Philadelphia: Government Printing Office.

Pope, C. (1995). Juvenile justice in the next millennium. In J. Klofas & S. Stojkovic (Eds.), *Crime and justice in the year 2120* (pp. 100–120). New York: Wadsworth Publishing.

President's Task Force report: Juvenile delinquency and youth crime. (1967). Washington, DC: U.S. Government Printing Office.

Regoli, R. M., & Hewitt, J. D. (1994). *Delinquency in society: A child-centered approach.* New York: McGraw-Hill.

Riley, R. (1994, May 12). Celebrate Goals 2000! *Teaching K-8.*

Rosen, L. E. (1994). We need a positive perspective and leadership. *High School Magazine, 2*(1), 24–26.

Rothman, D. J. (1971). *The discovery of the asylum.* Boston, MA: Little, Brown.

Rubel, R. J. (1977). *The unruly school.* Lexington, MA: D. C. Heath.

Sadler, W. (1988). Vandalism in our schools: A study concerning children who destroy property and what to do about it. *Education, 108*(4), 556–560.

Safe Schools Coalition, Inc. (1994, Summer). *School intervention report,* 7(4).

Schmitze, W. T. (1993). *Law enforcement in California public schools by the year 2002.* Sacramento: California Commission on Peace Officer Standards and Training.

Sexton, P. (1961). *Education and income.* New York: Viking Press.

Shaw, C. R., & McKay, H. (1969). *Juvenile delinquency and urban areas.* Chicago: University of Chicago Press.

Sheley, J. F., McGee, Z. T., & Wright, J. D. (1992). Gun-related violence in and around inner-city schools. *American Journal of Diseases of Children, 146*(6), 677–682.

Shepherd, G. D., & Ragan, W. B. (1993). *Modern elementary curriculum* (7th ed.). New York: Harcourt Brace Jovanovich.

Shepphard, G., & James, J. (1967). Police — Do they belong in the schools? *American Education,* 25–32.

Shurtleff, N. (Ed.). (1853). *Records for the governor and company of the Massachusetts Bay in New England.* Boston: Author.

Sivard, R. L. (1989). *World military and social expenditures 1989.* Washington, DC: World Priorities.

Slawson, J. (1926). *The delinquent boys.* Boston: Budget Press.

Snyder, H. (1993). *Arrests of youth in 1991.* Washington, DC: U.S. Department of Justice, Office of Justice Programs, Office of Juvenile Justice and Delinquency Prevention.

South Carolina Department of Education. (1993, May). *School crime incidents in S.C. public schools, June 1991 through May 1992.* Columbia, SC: Education Information Services Report Series.

Southeastern Regional Vision in Education. (1993, March). *Reducing school violence.*

Spaid, E. (1996, January 24). Flying bullets put school up against a wall. *Christian Science Monitor,* p. 1.

Spring, J. (1989). *American education: An introduction to social and political aspects.* New York: Longman.

Spring, J. (1994). *The American school: 1642–1993* (3rd ed.). New York: McGraw-Hill.

Stendler, C. B. (1950). Class biases in the teaching of values. *Progressive Education, 27,* 123–126.

Stendler, C. B. (1949). How well do elementary school teachers understand child behavior? *Journal of Education Psychology, 40,* 489–498.

Stouffer, G. A. (1952). Behavior problems of children as viewed by teachers and mental hygienists: A study of present attitudes as compared with those reported by E. K. Wickman. *Mental Hygiene, 36,* 271–285.

Subcommittee to Investigate Juvenile Delinquency. (1977). *Challenge for the third century: Education in a safe environment — Final report on the nature and prevention of school violence and vandalism.* Washington, DC: U.S. Government Printing Office.

Taba, H. (1962). *Curriculum development theory and practice.* New York: Harcourt, Brace & World.

Task Force on Youth Development and Community Programs. (1992). *A matter of time: Risk and opportunity in the nonschool hours.* New York: Carnegie Council on Adolescent Development.

This fabulous century, 1920–1930. (1988). New York: Time-Life Books.

This fabulous century, 1940–1950. (1988). New York: Time-Life Books.

This fabulous century, 1950–1960. (1988). New York: Time-Life Books.

This fabulous century, 1960–1970. (1988). New York: Time-Life Books.

Thrasher, F. (1936). *The gang.* Chicago: University of Chicago Press.

Toufexis, A. (1992, November 23). When kids kill abusive parents. *Time,* pp. 60–61.

Trump, K. S. (1993). Effective school-safety and security programs. *Updating School Board Policies, 24*(4), 11–13.

Tursman, C. (1989). Safeguarding schools against gang warfare. *School Administrator, 46*(5), 8–15.

U.S. Commission on Civil Rights. (1967). *Racial isolation in the public schools* (Vol. II). Washington, DC: U.S. Government Printing Office.

U.S. Department of Commerce, Bureau of the Census. (1992). *Statistical Abstracts of the United States.* Washington, DC: U.S. Government Printing Office.

U.S. Department of Health, Education, and Welfare. (1977). *Violent schools — Safe schools.* Washington, DC: U.S. Government Printing Office.

U.S. House of Representatives. (1975). *Safety and violence in elementary and secondary schools: Hearings before a subcommittee of the House Committee on Elementary, Secondary, and Vocational Education.* (Subcommittee on Elementary, Secondary, and Vocational Education of the Committee on Education and Labor). Washington, DC: U.S. Government Printing Office.

Violence in schools. (1993, November 8). *U.S. News & World Report,* 31–35.

Vold, G. B. (1968). *Theoretical criminology.* New York: Harcourt, Brace & World.

Walker, D. (1968). *Rights in conflict.* New York: Bantam Books.

Walters, G., & White, T. (1989). Heredity and crime: Bad genes or bad research? *Criminology, 27*(3), 455–485.

Watts, B.C. (1938). *The out-of-school activities of pupils as related to the elementary school curriculum.* Unpublished Ph.D. field study, Colorado

State College of Education.

Weapon-carrying among high school students: United States. (1991). *Morbidity and mortality weekly report, 40,* 681–684.

Wilson, J. Q., & Herrnstein, R. (1985). *Crime and human nature.* New York: Simon & Schuster.

Wooden, W. S. (1995). *Renegade kids, suburban outlaws.* New York: Wadsworth Publishing.

Index

ABOUT THE AUTHORS

Gordon A. Crews is Director of Criminal Justice and Military Programs at the University of South Carolina, Beaufort. He is coauthor of *Faces of Violence in America* (1996).

M. Reid Counts presently holds the title of Lecturer at the University of Nebraska — Kearney.

ISBN 0-275-95842-6

DATE	ISSUED TO